Asteroids in Astrology 3

Cubewanos, Haumeids & other TNOs
Series: Asteroids in Astrology 3
Author: Benjamin Adamah

Lay-out: Sylvia Carrilho

ISBN 978-94-92355-64-5

Publisher:

VAMzzz Publishing
P.O. Box 3340
1001 AC Amsterdam
The Netherlands
www.vamzzz.com
vamzzz@protonmail.com

ASTEROIDS IN ASTROLOGY 3

CUBEWANOS
HAUMEIDS
& OTHER TNOs

Benjamin Adamah

VAMzzz PUBLISHING

LIST OF IMAGES

CONTENTS

G.ⁿ Mitelli F.

ASTROLOGO	MORTE
Le cose più recondite, e segrete	Mentre le stelle ogn'or misuri intento
Suelo d'ogni destin, sia buono, ò reo,	Astratto à preueder ciò che non lice,
E scopro con l'occhial del Gallileo	Non t'auuedi qua giù ch'urti infelice
Qante braccia di Coda han le Comete.	Ne la Pietra fatal del monumento?

INTRODUCTION

DISCLAIMER

Regarding astronomical data
The field of astronomy that deals with mapping Kuiper belt objects, including all the dwarf planets and asteroids discussed in this book, is constantly evolving. This means that the diameters and orbital periods of these distant objects are often revised. For the objects in this book, astronomical data from universities and specialized astronomy centers in the United States (JPC, MPC, and others), France, and Poland were used, as they were available at the end of May 2023.

Regarding this series of books on asteroid astrology
As an astrologer, I remain politically neutral. Literally, because I never vote. My general view on politics is that it is a bizarre phenomenon driven by distortions and excesses that play out within the Cancer-Capricorn axis, with the negative side of Saturn prevailing in both the camp of political leaders and voters (shifting responsibility onto others). I can summarize my view on politics with the words of Groucho Marx:

> *"Politics is the art of looking for trouble, finding it everywhere, diagnosing it incorrectly and applying the wrong remedies."*

I mention this because, although some of my pieces may appear politically engaged, I am *apolitical*. The tragic aspect of our contemporary zeitgeist, distorted by the mass media to its very core, is that nearly everything you write or speak about is immediately politicized, fueled by an epidemic of identity crises. However, as spoken, this is nothing more than a hysterical zeitgeist phenomenon, from which I have distanced myself from the beginning. You can write about politics or political players without being political or taking a stance other than a human standpoint.

From an astrological perspective, every individual is equally interesting, regardless of what they do or how society judges their behavior or position.

In my work, I may have broken taboos by assigning dominant influence to certain asteroids in people's horoscopes, which, according to mainstream societal norms, fall into the realm of excesses (porn-stars, political dissidents, criminals) or for which the mass media created a completely distorted but politically desirable image (various politicians, billionaires, etc.).

As an astrologer and a human being, I have a very simple ethical standpoint, which I can summarize in the belief that astrological influences are nothing more than a necessary filter through which divine spirit and creative energy fragment, allowing creation to come into being. Within this mystical occurrence, where light divides and condenses kaleidoscopically into the manifest microcosmic world, I see astrology as an important tool for understanding this never-ending process.

These insights can help us create a world in which each individual can fully develop their core qualities, thereby experiencing maximum freedom and personal happiness. Thus, in contrast to the shadow of fatalism and determinism under which astrology has long been burdened, along with its divination aspect, I see astrology as an instrument that, through insights into and understanding of how intrinsic forces interact, can lead to more freedom and a higher level of human evolution.

CUBEWANOS OR CLASSICAL KUIPER BELT OBJECTS

A *Cubewano*, also known as a *classical Kuiper belt object*, is a type of Kuiper belt object (KBO) that orbits beyond Neptune **without** being influenced by an orbital resonance with Neptune. Unlike Pluto, Their orbits are relatively circular with low eccentricity and sometimes low inclination orbits in the range of 41-48 AU. These objects do not cross Neptune's orbit and have characteristics similar to the classical planets. The Cubewanos form a group of asteroids in the Kuiper Belt beyond the orbit of Pluto. Their orbital period around the Sun is 260 to 330 years. To be classified as a Cubewano, the asteroid must be quite large (at least about 100 km in diameter), although Arrokoth (36 km) is also recognized as Cubewano.

The name "Cubewano" comes from the first trans-Neptunian object (TNO) discovered after Pluto and Charon, which was initially designated as (15760) 1992 QB1 until it was named 15760 Albion in January 2018. Other similar objects found later were often referred to as "QB1-o's" or "Cubewanos" in honor of this object. While the term "Cubewano" is commonly used among those who practice new astrology, the scientific community more frequently uses the term "classical Kuiper belt object" to refer to these asteroids and dwarf planets.

Cubewanos in astrology: zeitgeist-dwarfs

Cubewanos are complex objects, mainly due to their versatility rather than inherent conflicts or wounds, as found in Centaurs and Jupiter Trojans, or the obsessive tendencies seen in Plutinos. Many of these objects are linked to the zeitgeist phenomena that characterize the 21st century. For instance, Quaoar governs growth and expansion through wiki-like structures and networks, which we encounter frequently on the internet. Albion represents the connections between previously separate areas or dimensions, emphasizing interconnectivity in general, and is also associated with the internet. Makemake governs new technology, microbiology, satellites, skyscrapers, peak performance, and experiences in various fields, including unique vocal ranges like that of soul singer Chaka Khan, with her Moon/Makemake conjunction. Praamzius is a complex Cubewano with a connection to weather, the wave-particle duality and analogous situations. Logos-Zoe resides in the world of spreadsheet planning, where the right hemisphere has minimal input. Varuna governs significant events in mass media that linger with the public, while Varda represents forceful expression, pounding the table to make a point forcefully.

The term "Cubewanos" encompasses a considerable number of dwarf planets or potential dwarf planets. While many are associated with postmodern or 21st-century phenomena and realities, they can also have a significant personal impact. The rules for Cubewanos in a chart, whether personal or mundane, are similar to those applied to most asteroids and dwarf planets: using orbs of just 1 degree is recommended, preferably even less!

Haumeids act like a mix of a Centaur and Plutino

This 1 degree orb-guideline also applies to objects mentioned in this book that may not be categorized as Cubewanos but rather as *Twotinos* and other objects (in deviant resonances with Neptune) or the *Haumeids*. Speaking of the latter, Haumeids, in general, are less concerned with collective developments, trends, and evolutions, focusing primarily on personal depth-psychological aspects, struggles, and drama. One could characterize them as behaving like hybrids between Centaurs and Plutinos.

CUBEWANOS

15760 ALBION
Emancipation, bridge builder, time bridges.

Cubewano 1992 QB1 was officially named Albion on January 31st, 2018 (over 25 years after its discovery) after a mythical figure from the works of William Blake. Albion measures 167 km in diameter and was discovered by David C. Jewitt and Jane X. Luu as the first TNO (Trans-Neptunian Object) after Pluto on August 30th, 1992 – the same year that the first photo was uploaded to the World Wide Web, the first www-server outside of Europe was activated, and Windows 3.1 and Windows for Workgroups were launched. Sir Tim Berners-Lee, the inventor of the World Wide Web, has Albion conjunct Damocles/2002 VE95 *(abrupt, great change that expresses itself creatively and/or addictively)* in the sign of new horizons and high-tech, Aquarius. Albion marked a new era in astrology as it serves as the starting gun for an unstoppable wave of new astronomical discoveries and astrological exploration.

Ellen DeGeneres, who did a lot for the emancipation of homosexuality, has Albion in conjunction with Gonggong or Snow White *(groups, group consciousness)*. Martin Luther King had Albion conjunct Psyche *(inspiration)*; sextile Chaos *(chaos, something to be healed)* and square Uranus *(at odds with the status quo)* and Cyllarus *(racism)*. His Achilles' heel was his dealings with women (square Cassanova). Transhumanism advocate Richard Dawkins has Albion conjunct Pholus/Silly/Lugh/1993 SB/1998 WW24; square Varuna/Hylonome/Sedna; opposition Utopia.

Albion seems to be mainly concerned with two overlapping things:
1. taking a powerful stance/ideal within the context of an emancipation process; 2. forming a bridge between two eras or worlds or cultures.
There is also a weak link with the occult and techno-occultism. Often, but not necessarily, new technology plays a role in this, and sometimes Albion shakes things up to get the process going. A special place is reserved for gay emancipation here. Albion also seems to be the bridge builder between the pre-internet period and the internet age.

In its deepest essence, Albion represents the dichotomy of Anrta and Rta, or the process of overcoming this tension. In the tantric philosophical tradition, Rta and Anrta are two important concepts that relate to the cosmic order and the forces of chaos and disorder. Rta refers to the natural order and harmony that pervades the universe. It is often associated with the idea of truth, righteousness, and morality, and is believed to be the guiding principle behind the workings of the cosmos. According to tantric philosophy, living beings can align themselves with Rta by living in harmony with the natural order and following ethical principles. Anrta, on the other hand, refers to the forces of chaos and disorder that disrupt the natural order of the universe. It is often associated with falsehood, deceit, the artificial, and immorality and is believed to be the result of human ignorance and selfishness. According to tantric philosophy, living beings can overcome the negative effects of Anrta by cultivating awareness and knowledge and by living in accordance with the principles of Rta.

The term "Cubewano" for a classical Kuiper belt object comes from the vocalization of QB1, the first of this group to be discovered.

The orbital period of Albion is 291 years and 47 days.

148780 ALTJIRA

Psychospheric and morphogenetic consciousness; tirauclairism; magic; contact with dream world and subconscious forces and currents; understanding of creative processes.

Altjira was discovered on October 20, 2001 by Marc W. Buie. It is a binary Cubewano, with two bodies orbiting a barycenter. The first body may have a diameter of 140 km and the second, S/2007 (148780) 1, measures 160 km. However, there is still a lot of uncertainty about the exact dimensions at the time of writing. Sizes of 201 km and 246 km are also mentioned.

Altjira is named after the primary creation god of the indigenous Australian Arrernte (also known as Arrarnta, Aranda, or Arunta) in Central Australia and the Northern Territory. According to their legend, Altjira created the Earth and everything that humans would need, but then withdrew without leaving any instructions. However, the world he created was very happy and slept in the Dreamtime, in which the first spirits simply dreamed away their problems. The Aboriginal Dreamtime is similar to *Yetzirah* of the kabbalists, the *Mithal World* of the Sufi mystics or Rupert Sheldrake's *morphogenetic field*, in which things exist in *potential meme form* before they actualize in the sensory/material world. However, the term Altjira is also used for places and locations in the land where the uncreated creation spirits, ancestral totem spirits, or genii loci (spirits of a specific location) reside.

Altjira is difficult to interpret in forensic mundane horoscopy, at most it serves as an indicator for something that is forthcoming but has not yet been actualized or concretized, and sometimes as a reference to a spirit, atmosphere, haunted house, or a place that is energetically and psychospherically charged. In the personal chart, Altjira is mysterious but clear in meaning. The characteristics of a dominant Altjira include: magic, magical awareness; psychospheric consciousness; high psychospheric intelligence and empathy; awareness of morphogenetic processes, the workings of memes, thought-forms, constructs, and the magical use of imagination techniques to effect change; chakra and energy body awareness; a great sense of form, taste, and color; sensitivity to sound and radiation fields; ongoing (shamanistic) contact with the subconscious and the collective unconscious, earth energy, genii loci, psycho-energetic recordings in buildings or objects; a built-in detection system to detect things that exert influence from the astral or energetic realm in others and in oneself; detection of obsessors and obsessions or susceptibility to them; hypersensitivity to psychospheric and morphogenetic consciousness; clairvoyance; magic; contact with the dream world and subconscious powers and currents; insight into creative processes or mastery of them; special connection to nature and sometimes magical connection to animals and plants; daydreaming or special nocturnal dreams; dream interpretation talent through an innate intense connection to the dream world and dream symbolism; issues with spirits, djinns, Elementals, or other beings in positive or negative ways; clairvoyance (magic that works with entities through invocation or evocation); a sense of natural spirituality and the natural order of things and creation, and a deep understanding of creative processes, either cognitively or intuitively or both; reality creation; making dreams come true; being dreamy or slipping into a dreamy state during the day; working remotely; problems with the "everyday reality"; understanding and grasping what one has made into a reality mode and distinguishing between this mode and the natural reality mode; alienation or loneliness due to not being able to match an artificial reality; aversion to the rat race, aversion to the domination and intrusiveness of technology and bureaucracy; very deep intense feelings that are sometimes difficult to put into words because the emotional perception is primarily connected to intuition and requires effort to translate into cognition; interest in spiritualism, seances, ghost stories, the afterlife;

contacting the afterlife; thinking a lot about the beginning and end of life or being strongly marked by the beginning of life; love for indigenous peoples; visionary; sensitive to the spirit of the times.

Altjira is a highly magical Cubewano, much like Deucalion. Deucalion has a particularly strong link with directionism, meaning the ability to give a magical command, or in other words, to generate a ripple effect in the time/space/consciousness/energy continuum. Deucalion has more of a Plutino-like nature. Altjira, on the other hand, is more Neptunian in nature and rules over the magic that carries out commands through entities. It encompasses the total psychospheric awareness of natural and supernatural forces, processes, and beings.

The orbital period of Altjira is 294 years and 35 days.

486958 ARROKOTH

Need for attention, and also fear of it; simulated reality; exposing disinformation; exposing the coordinates and structure of simulated reality or the political space and contrasting it with natural reality; interest in unusual or apocryphal technologies and phenomena (orgone, UFO's, VRIL, metaphysics, etc.); unusual networks; a mythical place beyond the known world; other dimensions; detecting emotional blackmail after having been wounded or terrorized by it for years or decades; bringing thoughts and feelings into synergy.

Arrokoth, also known as provisional designation 2014 MU69 and previously nicknamed *Ultima Thule*, is a trans-Neptunian object located in the Kuiper belt. The name Arrokoth was chosen to represent the Powhatan people indigenous to the Tidewater region of Virginia and Maryland, and it means "cloud" in the Powhatan language. On January 1, 2019, the NASA spacecraft New Horizons conducted a flyby of Arrokoth, making it the farthest and most primitive object in the Solar System to be visited by a spacecraft. Arrokoth is classified as a cold classical Kuiper belt object with a low orbital inclination and eccentricity. It is a contact binary, made up of two planetesimals that are 21 and 15 km (13 and 9 mi) across and joined along their major axes, with a length of 36 km (22 mi). Astronomer Marc Buie and the New Horizons Search Team discovered Arrokoth on June 26, 2014, using the Hubble Space Telescope.

Features: A strong drive to achieve greatness and gain admiration from others; the belief that success is the only way to earn love and respect; a domineering, controlling, or abusive father figure; tending to underestimate oneself and lack self-confidence; insecure and shy as a child, while these feelings can carry over into adulthood; a need for attention, and also fear of it; coming across as arrogant and egotistical, often as a defense mechanism to cover up deep insecurities; difficulties with admitting vulnerabilities to themselves, let alone others; outgoing and charismatic, and tending to be very popular, particularly with the opposite sex; addiction to risk and drama; a glamorous and elegant person, with an innate sense of style and charm; rebellious; resistant; does not accept being repressed or controlled; loves freedom but has some internal crisis to overcome and should guard against projection; outlaw; fighting in courtrooms or with lawyers to get justice; a crisis of belief is turned into a fight against the system; research journalism; exposing disinformation; exposing the coordinates and structure of simulated reality or the political space and contrasting it with natural reality; death or purging of one's arrogance; sudden death in conflict; learns to balance the personal "I want" with the mutual "we have to" via the ripening of emotional intelligence; interest in unusual or apocryphal technologies and phenomena (orgone, UFO's, VRIL, metaphysics, etc.); unusual networks; a mythical place beyond the known world; other dimensions; detecting emotional blackmail after having been wounded or terrorized by it for years or decades; first sexual contact of a male homosexual; racism issues; bringing thoughts and feelings into synergy; inclined to fears and the never-ending overcoming of fears; feelings of loneliness; learning to accept and love oneself and people in general; Amor fati; understanding that the limitation of ones talents is the greatness of ones talents; true non egotistical self love becomes a turning point in ones life; becoming popular as a (rebellious) writer.

Before this small peanut-shaped Cubewano was baptized Arrokoth, NASA asked the public for suggestions on a nickname for the object – before the flyby on 1 January 2019. On 13 March 2018, they chose "Ultima Thule" as one of the options. Thule, which means the northernmost location in ancient Greek and Roman literature and cartography, had acquired a metaphorical meaning of any far-off place beyond the "borders of the known world" in classical and medieval literature. When it was discovered that the object was a *bilobate contact binary*, the New Horizons team referred to the larger lobe as "Ultima" and the smaller lobe as "Thule". The lobes are now officially named "Wenu" and "Weeyo", respectively.

Arrokoth is neutral when it comes to good or evil, but can manifest in extremes on one side or the other. On the positive side we find for example

UFO-researcher Dr. Stephen M. Greer (known, among other things, for the documentary *Sirius* about an alien body found in the Chilean Atacama Desert). He has Arrokoth square Uranus/Makemake *(reaching the top in something extraordinary)* exactly at 27 Libra, square the Plutino 1996 SZ4 in 27 Capricorn *(a picture says more than a thousand words)*; in opposition to Sedna in 27 Aries *(lifting consciousness out of the matrix)* and sextile the Lunar Nodes/Galactic Center in 27 Sagittarius *(karmic destiny)*. Here Arrokoth is all about a deeper undersanding of reality and expanding our consciousness.

On the negative side we see oppressors who do everything in their power to overrule reality with a simulation model based 100% on lies spread by the media and politicians in their service. Bill Gates has Neptune conjunct Arrokoth *(simulated reality)* in 28 Libra, sextile Jupiter/Pluto-Charon/Haumea/2002 PN34 *(optimistic expansion of powerful parasitism)*. He is supported by the Sun in 6 Scorpio, which is in exact opposition to Amycus in 6 Taurus *(power abuse)*, and the Moon in 9 Aries, which is conjunct (2 arch-minutes exact) Eris *(persistent evil, rape of all human values)*. Bill Gates, who was one of the organizers of Event 201 (a simulation of the disinformation-tactics and strategies to launch the "covid pandemic" as the new simulated space). He bribed numerous big newspapers, media organizations, and universities all over the world, and has proven himself to be a champion of disconnecting people from reality, which helps him escape lifelong imprisonment in India or West Africa or, since the plandemic, anywhere else in the world. His Event 201 colleague Klaus Schwab has Arrokoth in 9 Libra in exact opposition a Saturn/Sun/Amycus conjunction in 9/10 Aries *(simulated space enforcement with the help of officials and the military)*.

Arrokoth has an orbital period of approximately 298 years.

66652 BORASISI-PABU

True or false issues; freedom from lies and appearances, or instead getting caught up in illusion; mechanical submission to a religious network or helping to expand it, or rather, piercing through religions to expose flaws and insecurities in career and identity in contrast to outward presentation; balancing act between duty and pleasure.

Borasisi, officially known as Borasisi-Pabu, was discovered on September 8, 1999 by Chad Trujillo, Jane X. Luu, and David C. Jewitt. It is a binary Cubewano. Borasisi measures 126 km and Pabu 105 km in diameter. The Cubewano was discovered on September 8, 1999. Borasisi-Pabu is named after a fictional creation god from Kurt Vonnegut's novella *Cat's Cradle*. In the story, Borasisi is the Sun and Pabu is the name of the Moon. Borasisi, the Sun, held Pabu, the Moon, in his arms and hoped that Pabu would bear him a fiery child. But Pabu only gave birth to children who were cold and could not burn. Pabu was therefore cast out, but then lived with her favorite child, Earth. In interpretation, Borasisi-Pabu seems to revolve around true or false, reality or illusion.

Characteristics include: free from lies and appearances; getting caught up in illusion; mechanical submission to a religious network or helping to expand it, or on the contrary, poking through religions; commercial religion; the money-grubbing and hypocrisy of the Vatican; criticism of science or blindly going along with sponsored science at the expense of truth-seeking; soulless engineering or technology or becoming aware of it; crisis or depression associated with a realization of a reality that turns out to be a sham; flaws and uncertainties in career and identity versus the presentation to the outside world; a dilemma between duty and pleasure; can react strongly, aggressively, or very resolutely when freedom is restricted or goals are thwarted. Borasisi can also create a feeling of being torn between work, obligations, and possibly an ongoing influence from a strict upbringing on one hand, and on the other hand a desire for relaxation, friends, going out, relaxing, and enjoying life. This often carries an irrational sense of guilt or some other inhibition. In extension, there is a desire to withdraw from the rat race or the suffocating system in which one moves.

Someone with a positive dominant Borasisi will demand more and more clarity and insight for themselves, missing it until they draw from their own originality and logic. The purging process preceding this will typically involve the scientific consensus aka academic 'truths,' religion or spirituality, or objectives that have a social status but lack a soul.

The orbital period is 287 years and 164 days.

19521 CHAOS

Autonomy, expressive power, originality; to be independent of recognition; embracing chaos as a "gap, abyss".

Chaos was discovered on November 19, 1998 by the Deep Ecliptic Survey (DES) and measures approximately 612 to 665 km in diameter. Chaos is a very powerful Algol/Scorpio-like energy that is bound by an important rule in order to thrive instead of derail: when there is a dominant Chaos in the natal horoscope, one must do passionate, driven work that they feel compelled to do, WITHOUT ever worrying about recognition. This is a difficult task, as almost nobody can sustain doing a lot of work without a pat on the back or positive feedback, but these things can paradoxically be expected with Chaos, only after one does not place any value on them and they are not part of the superdrive that this Cubewano can provide. This is partly due to the dichotomy between Mars in the 12th house of the discovery horoscope, along with the discovery of Chaos itself conjunct the star Algol, and the rest of the horoscope where there is an enormous will to do, self-expression, and a drive to reach the top. On the other hand, Chaos is strongly influenced by the inconjunct Saturn in Aries, conjunct the Sun/Varda/Moon in Scorpio. This is a difficult problem in terms of the parent-child relationship and later the relationship and balance between actions, ambition, achievement, and emotional security and comfort. Someone with a dominant Chaos usually has to seek and find this last aspect outside of the parental home base (where emotional security is often lacking), by creating their own "home". This is very important for this highly potential but difficult-to-handle Cubewano. If this is not achieved, Chaos usually focuses on being anti-authoritarian for the sake of being anti-authoritarian, which is a huge waste of energy.

Keywords: Impact; pillar that cannot be ignored, lightning strike; stirring something up, avalanche arrows, avalanches; capable of great achievements as a writer and thinker; writing talent, the possibility of becoming wealthy as a writer; photography talent; talent for combining images and text; driven by the feeling of being touched by a divine spark, seeing the divine beyond illusions of the zeitgeist and wanting to communicate it; ambitious, driven and inspired; Algol-like: great unrecognized talent, an image that works against them, feared due to the unconscious awe they invoke or the penetrating scope they have, desiring to enter the Sun, using great originality, originality and creativity to step out of the margin and shadow, projected images by others that do not match the true nature of the person; a Scorpio-like all-or-nothing passion, especially with conjunction of Chaos and Moon; rebelling against their

own fate; anarchistic, independent thinker and decision maker; autonomous, autonomy; transformative; dissatisfied with reality modification/zeitgeist in which they feel embedded and stifled; extreme achievements; endurance tests that are impressive but ultimately harm the nervous system or cause other, sometimes serious psychosomatic disorders; heroic personality; active, productive, forceful; difficulty with groups, group behavior and working with groups; difficulty finding a hearing with the masses; great emphasis on and energy put into personal expression, occasionally provocative or criminal; health issues, with afflictions – and stifled self-expression and freedom of movement – increased risk of heart problems, back problems, disorders of the reproductive organs, nervous system, panic attacks, hypochondria or exhaustion, usually as a result of obsessions and inability to put into perspective and temporarily distance oneself from their own ideals, aspirations and drive.

Chaos also represents: subjective, sharp, honest or forced desire to make an impression or impact without it serving any purpose other than that tendency itself; exaggeration, misplaced optimism or sharp criticism of others; a combative, purposeful, offensive way of thinking; the willingness to announce bad news, even when negative or when others look away, without hiding things; a strong desire for intense sexual experiences, sometimes unconsciously driven by a need for kundalini stimulation in relation to creative drive and stress on the nervous system; liberal or nonconformist views on sex; a greatly increased libido when in a positive flow; an allergy to lies; an ability to see through lies or, in some afflictions, a good ability to lie oneself, which is relatively rare in Chaos when it concerns a more intellectually developed person; a strong sense of justice; a chance of paranormal experiences or phenomena, specifically in one's own home, childhood, or at the end of life.

Forensically: punk, the punk movement, punk music; times with an increased level of rebellion like the 60s, 80s, and the infowars period from 2002 to the present; relationships that only work if there is a spiritual common ground; relationships with a wealthy partner.

Finally, it is crucial with Chaos that all visions, ideas, and creative goals that bring this force to the surface are checked for their reality content. This does not mean that someone with strong Chaos should conform to prevailing consensus, as Chaos can be a useful crowbar that creates space and freedom from constraints. However, the Saturn square Neptune in the discovery horoscope demands this simply. With a more realistic insight, the visionary and creative actually increase, even though it may feel the other way around.

A sudden acceleration in work and ambition is then possible. Russian researcher Gennady Maslov links Chaos to the outbreak of a disease, medication, or epidemics. I suspect that there is a correlation here between suppressing Chaos energy, which is far too intense to keep within any personal or culturally closed system, and its outbreak simply through illness. Maslov notes that both Vincent van Gogh and Friedrich Nietzsche had an exact conjunction of Chaos-Moon in their natal horoscope.

The orbit time is 309 years and 336 days.

53311 DEUCALION

Magical materialization; magic stone in the pond effect; chaos magic; natural magical ability; ability to give magic commands (directionism); sometimes tough stance, inflexibility; stopping water damage or ending vague situations; survival talent; authority; endurance; individuation.

Deucalion was discovered on April 18, 1999 by the Deep Ecliptic Survey (DES). The Cubewano's diameter is still uncertain, with estimates ranging from131 to 212 km. Deucalion was named after Deukalion, the mythical Greek version of Noah. After the great flood in which all people drowned, except for Prometheus' son Deukalion, Epimetheus, and Pandora's daughter Pyrrha, the goddess Themis tells them in an oracle to throw the bones of their mother behind them. When they realize that their mother is the Earth and her bones are stones, they throw them over their shoulders, and new people spring forth from the stones to repopulate the world.

In Deucalion's discovery horoscope, the Sun is conjunct Haumeïde 1995 SM55 *(conversion)* and Lucifer in the 29th degree of Aries, in which the asteroid Lucifer itself was discovered in 1964. The Moon is conjunct the star Algol and the Cubewano Chaos in the 27th degree of Taurus and sextile the metaphysical Plutino 1999 TC36. Mercury is exactly conjunct Hermes and the Aries point, and in a trine with Varda in the last degree of Scorpio, missing the exact conjunction by only two arc-minutes. Deucalion itself is in opposition to the Sun in the opposite sign, indicating an ambitious and goal-oriented nature.

Deucalion rules over magical materialization; the magical stone-in-the-pond effect; chaos magic; natural magical aptitude; being able to give a magical command (directionism); having a sometimes hard or inflexible stance; stopping water overflow or vague situations; survival talent; authority; endurance; and individuation.

It has always struck me that people with strong aspects to Deucalion often have a natural talent for magic and are very interested in it. Their main quality is what magic is essentially about, namely being able to change a situation, homeostasis, or life course at will in accordance with the true course of their individuation process. A curious nod to the myth is the conjunction of Ceto/Crantor in the discovery horoscope: the abrupt stopping of something watery or making it more concrete/focused by creating a "thelos" (meaning) for a mass of metacognitive information and energy.

The orbital period of Deucalion is 295 years and 295 days.

58534 LOGOS-ZOE
Beta-intelligence, calculating, (academic) rigor, linear logic.

Logos (actually Logos-Zoe) is a binary Cubewano, discovered on February 4, 1997, by a team at the Mauna Kea Observatory. Logos measures approximately 77 km in diameter and Zoe 66 km. Zoe is not a moon, but both bodies revolve around a barycenter. According to the discovery horoscope and test horoscopes, Logos has a cool, calculating power, as the name suggests. The Sun in the 16th degree of Aquarius, conjunct Vesta/Industria/Arachne and sextile Taurinensis, in combination with Mercury in Capricorn and the Moon in Capricorn in the first house square Saturn, with Orcus and Eris in a trine on the ascendant and the discovery Logos itself in the 6th degree of Virgo conjunct Echeclus; square Pluto indicates strong left-brain energy. Mars is in Libra in a trine with Uranus, sextile Chariklo and sextile Pluto. Saturn makes a sextile with Jupiter.

This indicates the following characteristics: concrete, down-to-earth, calculating, mathematical, balanced, emotionally cool, systematic, formative, analytical, linear logical, reasoning, rational, solid, reliable, detached, contemplative, academic. The downside of Logos is arrogance and self-righteousness from the haughty sense of superiority that people with high beta intelligence often exhibit, completely oblivious to the fact that this is ultimately just a narrow perspective, miles away from a fully developed perception of reality. A strong Logos can significantly "strengthen" the personality, similar to a Sun, Pluto or Saturn on the ascendant.

At the same time, Logos can seriously lack empathy, intuition, etc., while the emotional intelligence can be well below average and display a long learning curve in relational areas. Logos is certainly capable of creativity, but not in the realm of autonomous art or the like, but within the frameworks of technology, engineering, informatics, robotics, machine building, logistics, mathematics, astronomy, and other areas of knowledge. Logos implies an *academic* orientation, which has significant disadvantages. One never really gets to the subject or area being studied, but rather always circles it contemplatively, at a distance. This can lead to enormous mistakes and gaps in life, as well as strongly undermine the independence of the character and keep them always in a dependent position.

Logos may also express itself primarily financially oriented, which can only further entrench the situation. The conjunction with Vesta indicates that it is necessary, with a dominant Logos, to regularly distance oneself from the sterilized coolness of Aquarius and the material and money-oriented 2nd house. In case of affliction, Logos can cause digestive problems or complaints in the legs and hips. In transits, Logos works intensively, soberingly, calmingly, or contemplatively because one can suddenly look at something more dispassionately, or there is a kind of cold shower effect as with some Saturn transits. Looking at negative or stale emotional situations or ingrained habits and obsessions contemplatively, creating space, is a very useful and positive quality of Logos that can create new freedom and usher in a new phase of life.

The position of Logos in the natal chart indicates where one had difficulties expressing emotions or where one has gone through the necessary process on this level to overcome those inhibitions. At the same time, this position indicates where one naturally exhibits a kind of cool logic and authoritative judgments and perspectives.

The orbital period is 307 years and 153 days.

136472 MAKEMAKE

Technogeddon, "techno-rape," transhumanism, biohacking, IOT, vaccine-Molochs, satellites, skyscrapers, breaking height records in the broadest sense, masturbation, intrusion that the artificial makes into life.

Large dwarf planet and Pluto-like object (not a Plutino) in a 6:11 resonance with Neptune, discovered on March 31, 2005 by Michael E. Brown, Chad Trujillo, and David Rabinowitz, with a diameter (at the equator) of 1434 km and a rotation period of 22.48 hours. On April 26, 2016, it was announced that Makemake has a moon with a diameter of 160 km. The moon was named S/2015 (136472) 1 and MK 2.

Makemake encompasses a lot and capturing its essence seems very complex, but it boils down to an epicenter role in the process where technology (the artificial) collides with natural reality. Carlos Castaneda, expressing the vision of the Yaqui Indians, describes this process as the advance of inorganic life into the organic world. Many modern philosophers currently recognize something they describe as the advance of soulless sterile "things" into life, the world, nature, humanity, and human mode. Makemake seems to link or correlate itself to the epicenter of this process in an offensive and penetrating manner and to be the stealth leader of the transhumanist movement, the so-called *Fourth Industrial Revolution* and the poisoning of reality (by mass-media), industrial-political vaccination-marketeers (WHO, GAVI, WEF, UN, European Commission) and Earth through companies such as former Monsanto, Bayer, Syngenta, etc. Additionally Makemake is linked to microwave-pollusion via satellites, creating an unnatural semi-macrokosmos of fake-sphere. Satellites generally move in the layer of the atmosphere known as the thermosphere. The thermosphere is located above the mesosphere and extends approximately from 80 kilometers (50 miles) to several hundred kilometers above the Earth's surface.

Keywords: extreme performances in technology, engineering, computer science, and architecture, satellites, internet complexity; the IOT (Internet of Things); aimless technocratization, displacement of society, the rise of soulless things, inorganic life in Carlos Castaneda's definition, the penetration of the soulless or inert into the animate and living; extremes in modern and postmodern complexities and megastructures; genetic manipulation; robotization, automation; NSA, digital mass control, and resistance to it, talent in the field of computer science/internet/hacking; quantum computing (with Quaoar); epidemics and pandemics, swine flu, the Covid plandemic, depopulation, misuse of viruses for depopulation; virtual reality, infolepsis (neurotic addiction to non-formation through smartphones and tablets); fruit processing; outcasts, orphans, abandoned life, and also masturbation, sex with devices or machines, cybersex; chaos magic, artificial fertilization techniques, experiments on embryos. Makemake was exactly square to Jupiter in the 2020 New Year's chart, the year the world underwent a total social and physical rape orchestrated by the vaccine Molochs in collaboration with the Pentagon.

However, although Makemake currently seems to be associated with various, highly negative and threatening technological or digitally-driven processes, realized on worldly scale through mass impositions, Makemake itself remains neutral and usually restricts itself to indicating a peak performance possibility in a personal horoscope, as defined by its position and aspects in the chart.

I encountered Makemake several times during the launch of a satellite or the completion of an extremely high building that broke records. The height record seems to apply to everything. Queen of Soul Chaka Khan, known for the incredible range of her voice, has an exact conjunction of Makemake/Moon in Cancer, with only 2 arc minutes off, against the background of a very musical and sensual horoscope. The discovery ascendant and Moon of Makemake are in Sagittarius *(satellites, mega-skyscrapers)*; the midheaven in 14 Virgo *(chemical and pharmaceutical industry, physics, surgery)*; the Sun in the 11th degree of Aries, very close conjunction with Venus/Psyche/Zipfel in the 4th house; trine with Ixion *(complex processes, unethical or harmful inventions)*. The 11th degree of Aries is about wanting to control both humans, animals, and plants. The sextile that Makemake's natal Sun makes with Okyrhoe is almost exact, like the conjunction with Venus at 1.5 arc-minutes away, with Okyrhoe conjunct Tesla *(secret or apocryphal physics)*. The Sun is also conjunct within 1 degree with Mors-Somnus *(death and conspiracy related)* and in a very close opposition with Haumea/Rhadamantus/Chariklo.

NOTE: Despite its 6:11 resonance with Neptune, Makemake is officially clasified as a Cubewano.

Makemake's orbital period is 306 years and 44 days.

420356 PRAAMZIUS

The weather itself, climate, clouds; apocalyptic insights into worldly wrongdoings; perception resets; charting a new course and sticking to it.

Praamzius was discovered on January 23, 2012 by K. Cernis and R.P. Boyle and is estimated to measure a maximum diameter of 460 km. Praamzius comes close to a 3:5 resonance with Neptune, but falls just outside of it.

The Cubewano is named after the Lithuanian supreme god Praamzius. He was both the ruler of fate and time, as well as the Lord of the world, who ruled over Heaven and Earth, assisted by his children. All living beings and even all gods had to obey him and all his decisions were set in stone. Praamzius was aware of both the present, past, and future at the same time. Depending on the region, Praamzius had different names, such as *Dievas Praamzius, Prakurimas, Ikurejas* or *Sotvaras*, while in the western lowlands of Lithuania and in Prussia he was referred to as *Ukopirmas*. The main ritual directed towards the supreme god was performed during the winter solstice, and with the rise of agriculture, this ritual became increasingly important. The rites were permeated with archaic totems, animism, reverence for ancestral souls in the underworld, and took place for twelve consecutive days as a symbol of the twelve months of the year.

Praamzius has a kind of complexity and contemporary relevance that is normally only encountered with Haumeans. He was discovered conjunct the star South Ascellus *(fever, violence, accidents, eye problems, unpopular, and bad for business)* in the third degree of Aquarius *(imagination, fantasy)* on the midpoint of 1999 TB in Taurus *(thorough reality screening, scanning)* | 2004 EW95 in Scorpio *(apocalyptic visions)*; conjunct Veritas *(truth)* / Solidarity *(solidarity)*; square Jupiter, 1999 TB / Black Moon in Taurus *(purging financial and material reality)*. Skuld/Varda are conjunct the North Node in 14 Sagittarius, a degree that governs financial and economic affairs, activities and systems; Varda/Skuld provide direction for a homeostasis reset, involved in it, with great impact. Pluto is in Capricorn conjunct Arawn/Heracles *(powerful, resolute transformation of established reality, power construction)*. Mercury is trine Mars and Saturn is trine Neptune. Uranus is conjunct Ceres. In summary, Praamzius indicates a greatly heightened awareness of everything that needs to be addressed, made conscious and purged on a global scale (Taurus), particularly concerning the Earth itself, the socio-economic/financial situation and system (everyone has a right to a piece of prosperity or should have such a right). Praamzius is very visionary in this respect and has visions that, although they may seem apocalyptic, are pragmatic, confrontational and realistic.

Praamzius is a humanist who wants to liberate and improve, ecologically through new food sources and fossil reserves, energy supplies, but must confront the most indescribably filthy and dark abuses in the world concerning Mother Earth (osc. Black Moon in Taurus conjunct Asbolus/1996 TQ66/Sedna/Randi/Lust; opposition Machiavelli/Somnium/Summanus/Huya). However, because Jupiter is square the Sun, much energy is misdirected towards what is not important. In addition, the square of corrected Black Moon – Sun creates a strong aversion to confronting challenges, which can turn into survival behavior by putting Praamzius' energy in service of negative Scorpio traits: visionary talents in service of multinationals, governments, neoliberal companies and organizations, power institutions, established institutes. This is like patching portholes and straightening chairs on a sinking Titanic. And someone with a very dominant Praamzius will know this, even if they push it away.

Praamzius is primarily Aquarius-like, but unlike the usual airy nature, this Cubewano has an inseparable connection with removing anything that obstructs the positive forces of the Taurus sign (clean fertile planet, socially and materially just world). The Aquarian vision is used here for the benefits of Mother Earth.

Therefore, the positive Praamzius has immense visionary, reality-scanning ability, great imagination, and can address socio-economic and ecologically planetary issues and come up with solutions or at least be inspiring for new paths for the future. This positive Praamzius does not shy away from confrontation, even facing the most horrible abuses, from a deep knowledge that humans are capable of resetting the systems in which they work or are embedded, and resetting how they stand in reality and modifying it accordingly – and that this reality is not something that merely "happens" to them. The negative Praamzius ruins his environment and himself by avoiding confrontations out of cowardice. Praamzius has a strong urge for a summit, which can be achieved in two ways, but the path of least resistance will ultimately prove to be a dead end. In a metaphysical sense Praamzius rules the understanding of wave-particle and thought-focus interaction. Forensically, Praamzius has a link with the weather and climate in the broadest sense.

The orbital period is 277 years and 340 days.

50000 QUAOAR

The expansion of knowledge and organic development through a process that steadily forms a mycelium of growing networks and databases; wiki-like structures; the organic growth and development aspect of organons.

Quaoar is a dwarf planet with a diameter estimated to be around 1159 km, although there are multiple estimates. It was discovered on June 4, 2002, by Chad Trujillo and Mike Brown. However, there is a pre-discovery dating back to May 25, 1954. After Quaoar was found, old star photographs were examined to see if Quaoar appeared on them. Quaoar was found on photos from August 5, 2001, June 14, 2001, August 1, 1997, and May 17, 1983. This allowed for the precise calculation of Quaoar's nearly circular orbit.

After its discovery, Quaoar was initially referred to as "Object X" due to its unknown nature and potential large size, reminiscent of the concept of Planet X. Its actual dimensions were uncertain at the time, but its notable brightness led the discovery team to consider the possibility of it being the tenth planet. However, in July, the team utilized the Hubble Space Telescope to measure Quaoar's size, prompting them to explore potential names for the object, particularly those derived from local Native American mythologies. Adhering to the International Astronomical Union's naming convention for minor planets, which designates non-resonant Kuiper belt objects after creation deities, the team ultimately chose the name Kwawar (Quaoar). This name pays homage to the creator god of the Tongva people, indigenous to the Los Angeles Basin, where the California Institute of Technology, Brown's institution, is located. Quaoar has a moon named Weywot, which is about 100 km in diameter, fittingly symbolically named after the son of the Tongva creation god Quaoar.

In astrology, Quaoar is said to represent a creative Saturn. While Saturn essentially only represents a contracting and therefore shaping force, with all the psychosphere, phenomenology, and psychology derived from it, Quaoar forms a growing, evolving organon into a large, steady systematization or wiki-like knowledge structure. Where Saturn rules over the status quo, the old/current system, Quaoar rules over setting up, unfolding, and institutionalizing the new system or alternative system. Quaoar is also associated with the activating, stimulating system as opposed to the system that only restricts creativity and freedom. Of course, this also partly depends on the position in sign and house and the aspecting.

Quaoar is associated with growing organisms, organizations, biological growth structures such as forests, coral reefs, termite mounds, crystals in caves, social growth structures, city planning, new subcultures or art movements, new political or economic systems, new growth technologies such as the internet, Google, Wikipedia, new agricultural systems such as permaculture, growth cities, metro networks, rail networks, complex electronic systems, information systems, networks, etc. The focus in all of this is on the "logistics" of knowledge and communication structuring. Additional characteristics of the structures that Quaoar creates are their popularity and familiarity, their dependence, and their hidden shadow side, where investigative journalists, scientists, or other critics sometimes find it difficult to penetrate. Once large and powerful and embedded enough, negative Saturnine and Plutonic traits may emerge that tolerate no criticism.

A large part of the Quaoar organons has a relationship with power, and the structures themselves are a left-brain affair, a purely cognitive deprivation and processing of reality. This seems to conflict with describing Quaoar as a creative Saturn, but a creative Saturn is different from a creative Venus. At its discovery, Quaoar was in the first degree of Virgo, and the unfolding of a Quaoar structure therefore involves an unimaginable diligence, work drive, and eye for detail. However, this is limiting, if not threatening, to the development of all non-cognitive creativity and perceptions of reality, as well as holistic insights and crucial elements of humanity itself. For example, the NSA has a rather dark-aspected Quaoar (including conjunct Arachne/Hermes, opposition Crantor/Typhon, square Asbolus, square Machiavelli).

Quaoar has an orbital period of 288 years and 303 days.

120347 SALACIA
Sensual, artistic, magical, ebb and flow of lustful feelings; insights through drugs.

Salacia was discovered on September 22, 2004 by Henry G. Roe, Michael E. Brown, and Kristina M. Barkume, and measures 854 km in diameter. Salacia is a candidate dwarf planet.

In Roman mythology, Salacia was the goddess of saltwater and the wife of Neptune, the god of the sea. She was often depicted as a beautiful nymph or sea goddess, and together with Neptune, she ruled over the oceans and all its creatures. Salacia was associated with the calm and tranquility of the sea, contrasting with the more tempestuous and unpredictable nature of her husband. Though not as well-known as other Roman sea deities like Neptune or Triton, Salacia played a role in the mythological narratives surrounding the sea and water-related aspects of Roman culture. She was usually depicted under the name Amphitrite. Salacia has a moon, Actea, with a diameter of approximately 286 km, which orbits around her at a distance of over 5600 km.

Key concepts: Neptune-like, but has a more focused and optimistic energy of its own; flow; calmness; things that come easily; softness, a certain inclination towards the lighter side of life; understanding the difference between knowledge and wisdom, or not; moments of initiation; sensitive to astral turbulence; contact with the paranormal; chaos magic, the magical, delusions; illusions; sudden surges and declines of lust; ability to work inspired; distortion of perception; use of alcohol and drugs associated with insightful breakthroughs or fiascos; avoidance of confrontations; ostrich-like behavior or politics; musicality or artisticity; poetic; inspired or automatic writing; love and romance; psychospheric consciousness.

The composer Philip Glass, known for his unique music style with flowing melodies reminiscent of flowing water, has Salacia conjunct the centaur Narcissus; sextile Sun and Moon; trine Varuna/Circe; square Chaos. Matthew Manning, the British medium who became famous as a teenager for poltergeist phenomena and later automatic writing, has Salacia in the 7th degree of Capricorn in the first house conjunct uncorrected Black Moon, Nostalgia, Persephone and Lilith. Manning communicated frequently with past residents of his house, and hundreds of signatures appeared on his walls in sometimes centuries-old handwriting. An almost exact trine (within 1 degree) of Salacia-Varuna seems to have a strengthening effect on Salacia, positioning her even more as an active Neptune, with the humanistic and spiritual dimensions coming forward alongside the already known artistic and sexual ones. We find Salacia in the charts of porn stars Hotkinkyo and Jenna Haze, lodge head/ occultist and writer on magic Gregor A. Gregorius (with Salacia conjunct Mercury), writer Anita Moorjani (who came back from the dead and miraculously healed from cancer), mystic Carlos Castaneda, expressionist Jean Michel Basquiat, top psychic Anton Pauwe, director David Lynch, and NSA whistleblower Edward Snowden. Opera composer Richard Wagner (posthumously designated national composer in Nazi Germany) had Salacia in 17 degrees of Gemini conjunct Vesta; trine Germania; trine Moon; opposite Neptune.

Salacia in conjunction with the Plutino 1999 TC36 seems to promote astral travel and lucid dreaming. In combination with sexual or erotic asteroids or planets, Salacia works as a catalyst in this area: Egon Schiele (Salacia sextile Venus); porn star Cytherea (Salacia in three with Bacchus/Messalina); Jenna Haze (Salacia square 2010 EN65); erotic artist Franz von Bayros (Salacia trine Eros); erotic artist Hans Belmer (Salacia square Kaali and trine Fulvia, with Salacia conjunct Bienor/Meta). The genius expressionist and rock & roll singer Herman Brood had Salacia opposite ascendant/conjunct cusp7 and sextile 2010 EN65 *(orgasm, detonation/discharge)*. Brood painted extremely fast and generally under the influence of alcohol or drugs to afford his expensive, drug-soaked lifestyle. (See also the Plutino 2002 VE95 for Brood in my work on Plutinos in this series). An extremely strongly aspected Salacia is found in the charts of Carlos Castaneda and Sten Oomen (Out of Body expert). Salacia has a strongly anti-Saturnine nature. It is almost a kind of Neptune clone that apparently works very well with Varuna.

The orbital period is 273 years and 358 days.

79360 SILA-NUNAM
The smooth operator; incest issues; sexual trauma versus sexual pleasure.

Sila-Nunam was discovered on February 3, 1997 by Jane X. Luu, David C. Jewitt, Chadwick A. Trujillo, and Jun Chen. It is a binary Cubewano, with Sila (250 km), named after the Inuit sky god, and Nulam (235 km), named after the Inuit earth goddess, both revolving around a barycenter.

Its characteristics include: having good overview and keeping it; making thoughtful decisions; being able to manage difficult personal situations through discussion; embracing compromise; maneuvering processes in a flow; knowing when to keep distance; being patient; synthesizing; correlating; creating synergy; being visionary, empathic, and imaginative; being watery, associated with large bodies of water, the ocean; being fluid; managing flow or current; being involved in peace movements; and having an interest in the relationship between matter and spirit. Negative traits include: being diluted; allowing things that need attention or action to be neglected; losing control of situations; over-relativizing or trivializing; false pacifism; and, worst of all, incest and sexual trauma that makes sexual enjoyment difficult or impossible, which requires significant therapeutic intervention. Mark Andrew Holmes attributes to Sila-Nunam the following traits: long-term vision; being able to let things slide; serene acceptance; an easy-going and decadent attitude; and good listening skills.

Pax Christi Netherlands was founded with Sila-Nunam in Taurus conjunct Mercury *(peace talks)* opposite Chiron. Edward Snowden has Sila-Nunam conjunct Pandora (opened the NSA's Pandora's box). Mahatma Mohandas Gandhi, who used nonviolent resistance to change the entire political situation in India, had Sila-Nunam in a trine with Damocles *(abrupt and rigorous change via a short, effective chaotic phase).*

The orbital period of Sila-Nunam is 293 years and 7 days.

88611 TEHARONHIAWAKO

Profound and intense light-dark contradictions and dualities; unhappy marriages; reforms; seeing life as mission; paradoxes.

Teharonhiawako (actually Teharonhiawako-Sawiskera) was discovered on August 20, 2001, by the Deep Ecliptic Survey. It is a binary Cubewano where Teharonhiawako measures 220 km in diameter and Sawiskera measures 178 km.

Teharonhiawako and Sawiskera are deities from the mythology of the Haudenosaunee, also known as the Iroquois Confederacy. They play significant roles in Haudenosaunee creation stories and cultural beliefs. Teharonhiawako, also known as the "Sky Holder" or the "Holder of the Heavens," is a central figure in Haudenosaunee creation mythology. According to legend, Teharonhiawako worked alongside his twin brother Tawiskaron, also known as the "Flint" or "Holder of the Earth," to bring balance and order to the world. Teharonhiawako is associated with the upper world, the celestial realm, and the forces that govern the sky, such as the Sun, Moon, stars, and the cycles of nature. He is often depicted as a powerful and benevolent deity who provides guidance, sustenance, and harmony to the people. Sawiskera, sometimes referred to as Sawiskera Odoken or Sawiskera Ododoka, is another important deity in Haudenosaunee mythology. Sawiskera is a trickster figure and represents the chaotic and unpredictable aspects of life. As a shape-shifter, Sawiskera can take various forms and often plays mischievous pranks on other beings, including humans and other deities. Despite being mischievous, Sawiskera is also regarded as a teacher and a source of wisdom. The trickster figure challenges conventions and helps individuals learn important life lessons through unexpected and sometimes humorous situations.

Teharonhiawako was discovered conjunct Deneb Algedi and Uranus. Teharonhiawako was named after the supreme god of the Mohawks, and Sawiskera after his malevolent twin brother. Interestingly, the star Deneb Algedi also combines peaks of good and evil. Teharonhiawako rules over profound and intense light-dark contrasts and dualities. Other characteristics include: much sorrow; people involved in reforms; an imbalanced mind; people whose entire life is a mission, a personally made lonely struggle behind the scenes; occult accidents or blind spots, occult lodges or philosophies; tax problems; investment problems; an unhappy marriage and unhappy home situation; gaining respect and status, but without personal happiness; sexual scandals (especially in male horoscopes); a strange, peculiar, or violent death;

children involved with drugs. More generally, Teharonhiawako indicates paradoxes, dualities, black-and-white dichotomy, split or dual situations. The site astrologicaldepth.com finally links this Cubewano to something beautiful that is built up and suddenly ruined, yet still being able to laugh about it; jealousy issues; rebellion and living one's own dream.

A strong Teharonhiawako is found in the horoscopes of Nelson Mandela and Martin Luther King, where their great popularity (Hylonome) was in a trine aspect to Teharonhiawako and literally revolved around the unacceptable inequality between white and black. Martin Luther King had Teharonhiawako conjunct Wild sextile Sun; sextile Ixion/Bergvall/Klotho and square Skepticus/ Hexlein/house 11 cusp. Hylonome was conjunct Amycus in his chart. Mandela's Teharonhiawako in the 10th degree of Scorpio in the 11th house is aspected in conjunction with Salacia/Stampfer/Nietzsche/Eurydike/1995 QY9; opposition to 2001 KF77/Logos/Chariklo/Preiss/Seeberg; square to house 9 cusp; square to 2002 GZ32/house 3 cusp.

The orbital period is 290 years and 117 days.

174567 VARDA-ILMARË

Emphasis; impact; charisma; violent or violent outbursts originating from unconscious processes; actors and authors.

Varda or Varda-Ilmarë is a binary Cubewano. Based on its apparent brightness and assumed albedo, the estimated combined size of the Varda–Ilmarë system is 792, with the size of the primary estimated at 722 km. Varda-Ilmarë is possibly a dwarf planet and was discovered on June 21, 2003, by Jeffrey A. Larsen.

Varda-Ilmarë shares with the goddess from Tolkien the ability to give charisma (Brad Pitt), and a strong Varda-Ilmarë is a good predisposition for an aspiring actor or model. On the other hand, Varda-Ilmarë can also give violent outbursts and violent tendencies, as eruptions, arising from long-running farce situations in the unconscious that have not yet come to an end. In mundane astrology, Varda-Ilmarë is prominent in the horoscopes of attacks and violent outbursts. Varda-Ilmarë can also display fanatical political combativeness. Someone with a dominant Varda-Ilmarë can perceive the overload of technology in the postmodern world and its intrusiveness into human existence as very threatening, malevolent, and gloomy, and this coldness can stimulate a need for psychotropic drugs. Suicidality as a reaction to being overwhelmed by the advancing technologization and sterilization of the world also falls under Varda-Ilmarë. The energy of this newcomer is best expressed in acting or a writing career. Varda-Ilmarë stimulates the portrayal of intuitive, psychic, and psychospheric realities and truths in understandable language. The pen is the best channel for the inherent psychic and emotional fermentation processes. Avoiding inertia is the biggest challenge with Varda-Ilmarë. All forms of mental and emotional inertia are the basis of negative tension buildup in this Cubewano and block the very sparkling creative inspiration of the positive Varda-Ilmarë.

The orbital period is 313 years and 44 days.

20000 VARUNA
Super expansion; big, deep and long lasting impact through the media.

Varuna is a so called Jacobi ellipsoid Cubewano, suggesting that it has an elongated shape due to its rapid rotation. It has an estimated size between 678 km (diameter) and 1006 km (long axis). It was discovered on November 28, 2000 by Robert S. McMillan.

Astrologically Varuna is mainly about super-expansion, large media impact and fame, events that are not quickly forgotten and often the beginning of a decade-long popularity or notoriety, events that are known or remembered by a very large group of people, super-growth, mega-stars, international events, or historical milestones.

Named after the pre-Hindu ocean and creation god Varuna, this Cubewano seems to be an exponential magnification of Jupiter energy; impact; charisma; intense or violent outbursts originating from unconscious processes; actors and authors; super-expansion; deep and long-lasting impact via media in Gemini. Varuna is best expressed through the axis of the 3rd house - 9th house. It is a suitable Cubewano to work with in business astrology. The position of Varuna in the natal horoscope indicates where great expansion is possible. During the 9/11 attacks, Varuna was conjunct Jupiter/Hypnos *(hypnotic impact of a big event)*; square Ceto *(shocking media images)*. Varuna works on other bodies with which it aspects as an amplifier, manifestor, or empowerment, making it an important player in any horoscope interpretation.

Its orbital period is 279 years and 77 days.

UNNAMED CUBEWANOS

15807 1994 GV9

Over-detailed; soulmate desire; love/relationship issues.

1994 GV9 was discovered on April 15, 1994, by Jun Chen and David C. Jewitt. At the time of its discovery, it was located in the 23rd degree of Virgo, between the influence of the stars Denebola and Avior, conjunct Rhadamantus on midpoint Eros/Bowell|Neptune/Ambrosia (from two trines); opposition to Amor/Dimitrov; square to Aten. The discovery Sun is in Aries conjunct Circe/Itokawa/2002 VE95; opposition to Juno; square to Uranus/Neptune; sextile Typhon; sextile Manwë. The object has a diameter of 146 km.

Francesco Schiavinotto provides the keywords: precision, modernism, and meticulous (or petty) attention to details for 1994 GV9. However, the discovery chart also strongly indicates issues related to love, partners, and relationship problems. 1994 GV9 seeks the soulmate in preferably a life partner through many obstacles and pitfalls. Sometimes this Cubewano indicates a big gap between physical and mental/emotional love. If 1994 GV9 is heavily aspected, at some point a female spirit may force a breakthrough in a karmic process.

The orbital period is 291 years and 76 days.

15883 1997 CR29

Pursuit of a (financially) independent position; tendency towards financial short cuts; multi-level marketing.

1997 CR29 was discovered on February 3, 1997 by Chad Trujillo, Jun Chen, and David C. Jewitt. At the time of discovery, the object was located in the 16th degree of Leo, conjunct the star Duhbe, opposite the Sun, and has a diameter of 168 km.

1997 CR29 represents a creative and ambitious energy and vision, with a strong inclination to seek financial shortcuts such as multi-level marketing, etc. In the worst case, this may lead to financial crime or problems with gambling, and one may also become a victim of financial crime. The drive to become independent, which is often seen as based on financial independence, is very strong. Forensically, 1997 CR29 may refer to gas explosions or financial crime through pyramid schemes.

Its orbital period is 321 years and 274 days.

16684 1994 JQ1
Decoding; defragmentation, gestalt therapy; truth-seeking; wanting the real truth on the table rather than a politicized truth or tunnel vision ingrained in the public.

1994 JQ1 has a diameter of 183 km and was discovered on May 11, 1994 by Michael J. Irwin and Anna N. Zytkow. At the time of its discovery, 1994 JQ1 was located in the 29th degree of Libra, conjunct the star Izar (Belt of the Screamer) and the asteroids Wil and Minerva, opposite 1996 TL66, trine Aten/2003 CO1/Photographia in Gemini, and sextile Crantor/Pholus/Logos in Leo. The discovery Sun is in the 21st degree of Taurus, conjunct Chaos/ Cerberus/Cacus, square Borasisi/Icarus in Aquarius, and square Thalia/Elektra in Leo.

Symptomatic descriptions include: fighting for the truth; taking years to get the truth on the table; wanting the real truth on the table instead of a politicized truth or a narrow view that has been ingrained in the public; defending against lies or state lies with creativity, cunning tactics, and humor; being hindered by propaganda or falsely institutionalized official positions; waging a long battle against collusion; constantly being forced to deal with lies or government lies for one's own livelihood or to tackle them.

At its core, 1994 JQ1 is about decoding, the value of qualitative distinction in the quantitative, defragmentation, gestalt therapy, and general processes where the chaff must be separated from the wheat from a chaos of information, and the information must be rearranged so that the forest can be seen through the trees again. For example, in extensive police investigations of important cases or in forms of scientific research, explicitly related to topics where there is a lot of noise that must be eliminated or investigative journalism where the rubbish that official media outlets spread for governments and large companies, must be debunked.

Its orbital period is 294 years and 124 days.

19255 1994 VK8

Opposition to Orwellianism; organs, processes or persons suddenly eliminated; high-impact marriage; vetting or scanning of (flawed) systems of care.

1994 VK8, discovered on November 8, 1994 by Alan Fitzsimmons, Donal O'Ceallaigh, and Iwan P. Williams, has a diameter of 175 km.

Its interpretation indicates resistance against control systems, anti-Orwellianism, resistance against politicized control systems or misuse of them, scrutiny or scanning of (incorrect) care systems, sudden shutdown of someone or something, or skepticism toward inert systems. Forensically, 1994 VK8 refers to a marriage that has or had a significant impact, an execution, or a hitman.

Its orbital period is 280 years and 267 days.

49673 1999 RA215

Radicalism; extremism; violence; martyrdom; terrorist attack; the radical act or rupture; nuclear technology or accidents, nuclear scandals, nuclear disaster; aerial bombings; bombers; chemtrails; auto racing aircraft satellite or space flight disasters; death issues.

1999 RA215 was discovered on September 13, 1999 by Donald R. Davis, Brett James Gladman, and Carol Meese and measures 128 to 153 km in diameter.

In the radix horoscope, 1999 RA215 is an epicenter of radicalism or extremes in a positive or negative sense. In a positive sense, radicalism is sometimes necessary to break through a farce. 1999 RA215 amplifies and strengthens the planets, points, or objects with which it aspects. This object is of great mundane importance. The discovery horoscope of 1999 RA215 shows a cluster of extremes that, when added up, without a doubt point in the direction of: radicalism or extremism; violence; martyrdom; a terrorist attack; false flag attacks; the radical act or break; nuclear technology or accidents; nuclear scandals; nuclear disaster; air bombings; bombers; chemtrails; car race, airplane, satellite, or space flight accidents; death issues. In the most positive case, a strong 1999 RA215 in personal horoscopes can produce a civilized, humanitarian, and constructive anarchist, a radical but possibly exceptionally creative writer with a significant impact, or someone with a natural talent for magical directionism and chaos magic. 1999 RA215 struggles with extremes in the realm of identity and often expresses this very violently in the outside world because the outside world is usually perceived as a potentially invasive boogeyman, even if it doesn't actually behave that way towards the person in question. This is one of the most extreme objects among the newcomers in astrology.

The otherwise peaceful French anarchist Pierre-Joseph Proudhon had 1999 RA215 conjunct Pholus in Cancer, square Hylonome *(popularity due to anarchism that breaks someone apart)*; and trine Venus/Eros/Ixion/Cetus in Pisces *(an equally passionate and reflective social involvement with the less privileged, which has a backlash effect)*. He is known for the statement "Property is theft". Mundanely, 1999 RA215 has a strong link to a specific type of attacks and, between 1998 and 2027, particularly with state terrorism and Deep State corporate wars, on which the entire foundation of the US economy now depends.

This entire period remains under a high tension of a long-running conjunction between 1999 RA215 and 2003 OP32, as will become clear shortly within this context. All the attacks committed during this period have this conjunction in common (within 1 degree), but they also have their own horoscope that contains a strong trigger and further characterizes the attack.

During 9/11, 1999 RA215 was in the 17th degree of Aquarius in the 4th house *(homeland)* conjunct 2003 OP32 *(reinforcement of an off-the-grid opinion)*; trine Elatus in Gemini *(negative fusion to the terrorism issue in the context of freedom = Bush's version of Freedom & Democracy through the media)*; trine 2000 GN171 in Libra *(allowing power and influence problems to be fueled by partners, here, friendly states and CEOs)*; opposition Venus/Leviathan/Sophia/ Zero in Leo *(a big shining popular state lie brought forth as wisdom and ratified with Ground Zero)*; sextile 1993 SB in Aries in 7 *(Orwellian screening of the individual citizen in friendly and openly hostile nations)*.

During the attack in Brussels on 22-3-2016 (a classic Gladio/NATO attack orchestrated by the media as terrorism according to the Danish top specialist, Ole Dammegård), 1999 RA215 was in the 7th degree of Pisces also conjunct 2003 OP32 opposition Orcus *(death)*. Furthermore, 1999 RA215 was conjunct Rockefellia/Icarus *(inspired by big money)*; square Mars in Sagittarius *(intense publicity)*; square Asbolus in Gemini *(reporting of the appalling)*.

The same conjunction 1999 RA215-2003 OP32 in opposition to Orcus was present during the "attack" in Nice on July 14, 2016, by a completely confused man, but again sold to the public as "Muslim terrorism" by the media. The triggering function here is not Mars but Black Moon, which is in a trine to this conjunction from the 7th degree of Scorpio in the 8th house. Pallas *(politics)* was conjunct 1999 RA215/2003 OP32 at that time, hence the politicization of the man in the truck via the media went smoothly. The conjunction made a square with the 4th and 10th house cusps from the 8th degree of Pisces in the first house.

On December 12, 2013, a United States aerial drone launched four Hellfire missiles on a wedding procession convoy of 11 cars and pickup trucks in rural Yemen. The strike killed at least 13 men and wounded at least 15 others, 6 of them seriously (one victim more than during the white, European Charlie Hebdo-case). The Western (social)media remained silent – no Yemenite flags on Facebook – because Yemenite people are simply not white *(Mercury was inconjunct Cylarus, which indicates racism, not communicative, shared or experienced as racism)* nor rich, and thus not seen as human beings. The conjunction of 1999 RA215/2003 OP32 was conjunct Neptune *(blurring)*, a minute-exact square Asbolus *(appalling)*, and trine 1998 TD10 *(invasion)*/1998 VG44 *(state disinformation)*. The problem with the conjunction of the Cubewano 1999 RA215 with Haumeïde 2003 OP32 is that it is long-running. It is like a volcano where there is a constantly smoldering magma present that, in certain complex total horoscopes, is triggered to come out.

To a certain extent, the dark counterpart of the "hippie configuration" that emerged from the long-running conjunction of Orius/2003CO1, which inherently encouraged freedom, liberalization of the mind and the individual, ecological awareness, creative revolutions, and autonomy. 1999 RA215/2003 OP32 appears to have been realized, or rather pragmatized and caricatured, in the rollout of the PNAC (Project for a New American Century) agenda, the Orwellian repression plans of US puppet Brussels, and behind-the-scenes politics of Bilderberg, WEF, etc.

During the HAARP-induced Fukushima disaster (according the data of the Tokio based geomagnetic meter of that time) on March 11, 2011, 1999 RA215 was conjunct Neptune/Chiron square Moon/1996 TL66 *(tsunamis, watersheds)*.

The orbital period of 1999 RA215 is approximately 285 years.

DATE	1999 RA215	2003 OP32
01 Jan 1980	21 cp 37	12 cp 37
01 Jan 1981	22 cp 45	14 cp 19
01 Jan 1982	23 cp 52	15 cp 59
01 Jan 1983	24 cp 59	17 cp 38
01 Jan 1984	26 cp 6	19 cp 17
01 Jan 1985	27 cp 15	20 cp 58
01 Jan 1986	28 cp 23	22 cp 36
01 Jan 1987	29 cp 31	24 cp 13
01 Jan 1988	0 aq 39	25 cp 49
01 Jan 1989	1 aq 49	27 cp 27
01 Jan 1990	2 aq 58	29 cp 1
01 Jan 1991	4 aq 6	0 aq 35
01 Jan 1992	5 aq 15	2 aq 8
01 Jan 1993	6 aq 26	3 aq 42
01 Jan 1994	7 aq 35	5 aq 14
01 Jan 1995	8 aq 45	6 aq 45
01 Jan 1996	9 aq 55	8 aq 15
01 Jan 1997	11 aq 7	9 aq 46
01 Jan 1998	**12 aq 18**	**11 aq 15**
01 Jan 1999	**13 aq 29**	**12 aq 42**
01 Jan 2000	**14 aq 40**	**14 aq 9**
01 Jan 2001	**15 aq 54**	**15 aq 37**
01 Jan 2002	**17 aq 6**	**17 aq 2**
01 Jan 2003	**18 aq 18**	**18 aq 26**
01 Jan 2004	**19 aq 31**	**19 aq 49**
01 Jan 2005	**20 aq 46**	**21 aq 13**
01 Jan 2006	**21 aq 59**	**22 aq 35**
01 Jan 2007	**23 aq 14**	**23 aq 57**
01 Jan 2008	**24 aq 29**	**25 aq 17**
01 Jan 2009	**25 aq 46**	**26 aq 38**
01 Jan 2010	**27 aq 2**	**27 aq 58**
01 Jan 2011	**28 aq 18**	**29 aq 16**
01 Jan 2012	**29 aq 35**	**0 pi 34**

DATE	1999 RA215	2003 OP32
01 Jan 2013	0 pi 54	1 pi 52
01 Jan 2014	2 pi 11	3 pi 8
01 Jan 2015	3 pi 30	4 pi 23
01 Jan 2016	4 pi 49	5 pi 37
01 Jan 2017	6 pi 9	6 pi 52
01 Jan 2018	7 pi 29	8 pi 6
01 Jan 2019	8 pi 50	9 pi 19
01 Jan 2020	10 pi 12	10 pi 31
01 Jan 2021	11 pi 36	11 pi 44
01 Jan 2022	12 pi 59	12 pi 56
01 Jan 2023	14 pi 23	14 pi 7
01 Jan 2024	15 pi 47	15 pi 18
01 Jan 2025	17 pi 14	16 pi 28
01 Jan 2026	18 pi 39	17 pi 38
01 Jan 2027	20 pi 6	18 pi 46
01 Jan 2028	21 pi 33	19 pi 55
01 Jan 2029	23 pi 1	21 pi 3
01 Jan 2030	24 pi 30	22 pi 11
01 Jan 2031	25 pi 59	23 pi 18
01 Jan 2032	27 pi 29	24 pi 25
01 Jan 2033	29 pi 1	25 pi 32

February 1998 is the first month in which this conjunction is exact within 1 degree. On February 19, 1998, 39 American neoconservative signatories sent an open letter to the President of the United States urging him to attack Iraq. This infamous memo is actually the activation of the rollout of a sustained wave of state terrorism from the US/NATO to the rest of the world, through bombings, disruptions in domestic politics, and Gladio attacks sold by the mass media as Muslim terrorism. This period hypothetically ends in 2027, when the conjunction of 1999 RA215/2003 OP32 comes to an end. *(See 1999 RA215 page 41 and 2003 OP32 page 73.)*

55565 2002 AW197 (NAME SUGGESTION: BARKAS)

For the sake of love, harmony and preservation of nature in the world, putting things at risk; anti-mass hysteria, zeitgeist relativisation; super strategy and genius insights regarding balance restoration; the growth of shyness and otherworldliness towards holistic intelligence; major shifts, supercontingency; world karma.

2002 AW197 was discovered on January 10, 2002 by a team from the Palomar Observatory led by Michael Brown. At the time of its discovery, this Cubewano was in the 14th degree of Leo conjunct 2001 BL41/Cusp 11th house and has an estimated diameter between 768 - 886 kilometers.

Its interpretation suggests, with strong personal aspects, an intense perception and penetrating scope regarding major processes within the social and cultural environment, the zeitgeist, and the Earth that one feels embedded in, and is either swept along with or threatened to be swept along with. These processes are perceived intuitively and emotionally at a very young age, and later form a stronger grip within the mind. Great cause-and-effect patterns, which are blind spots for the masses, crystallize and thus the pulsating pressure of an often unbearable existential dissonance grows stronger and stronger until a parallel process of both the almost complete cognitive ability to handle it and a genius talent for creative strategy has matured into ideas for balancing, and the individual remains under this invasion pressure.

2002 AW197 is highly averse to any form of brainless and harmful mass behavior, mass hysteria, following (opinion) leaders, politicians, parties, gurus, and trends, and has a natural antenna for it long before things are mentally understood. When 2002 AW197 is conjunct the Sun, Moon, Ruler, North Nodes, or Ascendant, one typically develops from shyness and confusing otherworldliness into a highly philosophically and strategically informed personality and a formidable opponent when provoked by a group, system, authority, or government. In mundane astrology, 2002 AW197 points to major social shifts, school tectonic activities, global processes, world karma or supercontingency (large balancing corrections where things went awry), major eruptions or changes within the social, economic, ecological, or geopolitical/military environment. Francesco Schiavinotto links 2002 AW197 to earthquakes. In the discovery horoscope, 2002 AW197 has the Sun conjunct Venus/Pallas/Hidalgo in Capricorn, trine Ganesa; sextile Sphinx. The Moon is in Sagittarius conjunct Quaoar; sextile Damocles/Cusp 5th house. Mars is conjunct Vincequerra/Heracles/Industria in Pisces, and the Midheaven is conjunct Varuna/Jupiter in Cancer, trine Toro and trine Hylonome conjunct

Tyr/2001 KF77. Uranus/Teheronhiawako is in Aquarius in the 5th house, directly opposite Orcus in Leo in the 11th house, which links rebellion or eruption to tension caused by the societal pyramid top in relation to a drive to end the continuous dissonance between imposed ideals in service of the status quo/consensus, which the established power relies on, and the creative expression of the people themselves. Mercury is conjunct Neptune/Amor and forms a trine with Saturn and the ascendant/Haumea/Rhadamantus/2001 EW95/Standing Bear *(strongly inspired to stand up for the rights of Mother Earth from a very broad perspective)*. Under the rulership of Jupiter and Mercury (conjunct Neptune/Amor), Pluto is conjunct Rhiphonos/Hermes/Torricelli/Arawn in Sagittarius in the 3rd house, leading to continuous disruptions and turbulence concerning the course, aspirations, personal belief, or personal consensus, which require daring creative solutions from time to time. At the mundane level, this indicates severe, unpredictable communication and transportation disruptions or turbulence in the academic or religious world.

Crucial to the characteristics of 2002 AW197 are the conjunction of the Sun/Venus/Pallas/Hidalgo in Capricorn in the 4th house, with a hard square from Eris/Hilda/1995 QZ9/2001 UR163 in Aries in the 7th house, which translates into a constant need to defend against hostile invasive pressure and the triggering of a survival strategy that must be very rigorous. The strong aspects of Hidalgo and Damocles to the Sun and Moon, the Uranus aspect, and the Pluto/Torricelli conjunction make 2002 AW197 a very strong and active revolutionary force, combined with the Sun/Venus in Capricorn, which demands stability, oscillating between pressure building and eruption (contingency actions). Disorder is clearly inherent, but never the goal; the goal is to achieve a better order than the old.

Julius Evola ("Revolt against the modern world") had 2002 AW197 conjunct Mercury/Strong/Itokawa in Taurus; inconjunct Saturn/1998 BU48; square Asbolus/Randi/Industria; sextile the "whistleblower-Centaur" 2001 KF77; trine Skuld and opposite the metaphysical Plutino 1999 TC36. Rene Guenon ("The Reign of Quantity & Signs of the Times") had 2002 AW197 in Aries opposite Jupiter; inconjunct Sun; sextile Typhon. Alfred North Whitehead ("Process and Reality") had 2002 AW197 conjunct Neptune/Sedna/1999 CE119; opposite 1999 TC36; trine Industria; square Varuna/Hidalgo/Sethos; square Ixion (thus at midpoint Varuna/Hidalgo/Sethos|Ixion); sextile Chariklo and trine Nessus.

I suggest the name Barkas for 2002 AW197, as it was the surname of Hannibal, but Hannibal already exists as the main belt asteroid 2152. The reasons for Hannibal are the genius strategic insight and creative scope of this general, which perfectly match the characteristics of 2002 AW197.

The orbital period is 322 years and 237 days.

59358 1999 CL158

Cultural philosophy; fathoming the relationship between individual and zeitgeist; guarding the human and earthly measure, especially with regards to children; longing for an intimate soulmate relationship or ruining it with excessive idealism, spiritual delusions or addiction.

1999 CL158 was discovered on February 11th, 1999 by Jane X. Luu, Chad Trujillo, and David C. Jewitt, and is classified as an "unstable Cubewano." Its diameter is estimated to be 183 km. At the time of its discovery, 1999 CL158 was in the third degree of Leo conjunct Orius; opposite Neptune/1999 OY3; trine Chiron in Sagittarius; trine Pallas in Aries; sextile Rhadamantus in Libra. The discovery Sun in Aquarius is opposite the North Nodes. Venus in Pisces conjunct 1999 TD10 and trine Typhon in Cancer both aspect the uncorrected Black Moon. Mercury is conjunct Snow White/Bienor/Narcissus; sextile Saturn/Itokawa and trine 2001 KF77. Additionally, during its discovery, 1999 CL158 was conjunct the star Talitha, named after a dying girl who was healed and raised by Jesus' statement, "Talitha cumi" (Little girl, I say to you, arise!).

A dominant 1999 CL158 can be summarized as an aspiration to treat the Earth as if we are borrowing this planet from our children. This Cubewano, with dominant aspects, offers a natural cultural-philosophical insight into one's own time, sees blind spots in what progress must continue, is highly aware of the relationship and correlative bonds between the self and the outside world or zeitgeist, sees frictions therein, not only for oneself but also socially, ecologically, economically, technologically, and culturally. There is also a particular sensitivity to the rights of children and the way in which they are forced to undergo certain types of reality modification. It is a very special and positive Cubewano that remains faithful to the human measure and reason (the choice to be and remain a "Mensch" against all ods). In a horoscope of someone with writing talent, 1999 CL158 will not manifest itself as a classic whistleblower, but rather uncover a deeper layer and produce structural cultural philosophy that addresses the humanization of the individual and social climate in the face of dehumanizing currents in the zeitgeist.

The French cultural philosopher and rat race critic Jacques Ellul criticized modern society for degrading our reflective ability to mindless automatic reflexes as a result of a way of life that is far too fast, leading to everything becoming aimless. Ellul had 1999 CL158 strongly aspected in the 29th degree of Aquarius in a fascinating conjunction with Amycus/Atropos/Aten *(Atropos is associated with a nodding donkey, thus endless automatic repetitions)*; trine Pluto/Child in Gemini; sextile North Nodes; square Hidalgo/Mors-Somnus *(waking up sheeple)*; opposite Dimitrov *(emerging from a crisis)*.

Its orbital period is 269 years and 212 days.

79983 1999 DF9

Dramatically ending activism; campaigning against harmful technology; falling victim to reprisals as a whistleblower; being mangled by collusion forces.

1999 DF9 was discovered on February 20, 1999 by Jane X. Luu, Chad Trujillo, and David C. Jewitt and has a diameter of 265 km.

Characteristics: dramatically ending activism; campaigning against harmful technology; becoming a victim of retaliation by government, industry or secret service as a whistleblower; being squeezed by collusion forces. Forensic: activists and whistleblowers who become victims of their own integrity, humanity, sense of justice, and courage. This Cubewano focuses the drama on the Pisces-Virgo axis, thus addressing issues related to physical and mental health; technology and care versus ethics and holistic visions; the concrete versus the spiritual dimension; the right time for something to crystallize, i.e., be launched, announced, put on the market, put into use, etc. For example, 1999 DF9 could be about a whistleblower who exposes a prematurely launched and harmful medicine and is persecuted, framed (or worse) as a result.

Vladimir Zelenko (27 November 1973 - 30 June 2022) was a Ukrainian-American physician who gained prominence by proposing a combination of three medications – hydroxychloroquine, zinc sulfate, and azithromycin – for use as part of an experimental outpatient treatment for COVID-19 that he promoted as the "Zelenko protocol". In 2019, Zelenko co-authored a book on Kabbalah, Jewish mysticism, and Chassidism titled *Essence To Essence* with one of his sons, Levi Yitzchok. The book describes the metaphysical dynamics that are common in science, medicine, psychology, economics, law, and politics. Because of staying loyal to medical ethics and commons sense instead of worshipping Dr. Fauci, Bill Gates and the rest of the pandemic leaders he was continuously attacked by the Big Pharma sponsored media. Even posthumously wikipedia keeps throwing mud at this courageous and spiritually motivated physician. Zelenko had 1999 DF9 very strongly aspected in 25 Cancer conjunct Orcus *(stay loyal to ones principles)* in exact square to Mars/Chaos/Tyson/Midas in 25 Aries *(being aggressively and forcefully, actively attacked by disease-authorities with financial motives)*; square Hinderer/1994 JS *(very strong repression)* in 25 Libra; trine Panacea/Serendip *(finding an alternative medicine that gives relief)*; trine 1995 SM55/1998 WU31 *(a positive breakthrough, powerfully presented)* in 25 Pisces.

The orbital period of 1999 DF9 is 319 years and 43 days.

85633 1998 KR65

Intellectual crowbar; pulling out all the stops to realize a dream; intellectual dominance; passionate positive will; tendency to dabble; being able to put idealism in synergy with realism has a direct positive impact on cash flows; mental burnouts.

1998 KR65 was discovered on May 29, 1998 by Gary M. Bernstein and measures 192 km in diameter.

Characteristics: all or nothing; intellectual lever; doing everything possible to break through with an innovation, invention, idealism; doing everything possible to realize a dream; intellectual dominance, but based on integrity; a passionate positive will, which can however be overshadowed by a tendency towards fanaticism; the need to give up complacency or vanity; dissonance between intellectual ambition and emotional intelligence as a potential blind spot; bringing idealism into synergy with realism is directly of positive influence on cash flows and income, and vice versa, if the synergy fails, it is disastrous.

Forensic: people or animals breaking out (literally or figuratively); the great innovator or pioneer in the field of knowledge; the unrecognized genius; suicide of a life partner of the engineer/inventor type, whose efforts were not rewarded or accepted or who ran against the tide of consensus, while exacerbating the situation with their own fanaticism. With affliction, there is a great risk of mentally exhausting oneself completely and even continuing to work towards the ideal during a burnout because realizing this ideal is perceived as personal karma (both Lunar Nodes in the 30th degree of

Aquarius in the discovery chart). 1998 KR65 itself was in the 24th degree of Capricorn at the time of discovery under the influence of Terebellum.

The orbital period is 285 years and 164 days.

119951 2002 KX14

Learning to deal with criticism; reactions to criticism versus self-integrity; managing criticism positively and negatively; talent for bringing in money through partners or cooperation or by getting bribed.

Discovered on May 17, 2002 by Michael E. Brown and Chad Trujillo. Initially thought to be a Plutino, 2002 KX14 is now classified as a Cubewano since it does not appear to be in a 2:3 resonance with Neptune. Its estimated size ranges from 496 to 562 km in diameter, making it a large object.

2002 KX14 has a very complex discovery chart, but the interpretation points towards an "Angela Merkel-like" thick skin and strategic/tactical approach, as well as a talent for tapping into money flows through partnerships, collaboration, or contracts, particularly when Mars is well-placed and strongly aspected in the chart. Merkel has 2002 KX14 conjunct Pallas *(politics)*, square the ascendant and cusp 7, and trine Hylonome *(popularity)*. Francesco Schiavinotto has associated 2002 KX14 with remarkable work ethic, liveliness, modesty, and tolerance to criticism. While I believe this to be accurate, it is not the only characteristic of 2002 KX14.

In the discovery chart, the ascendant in Capricorn is conjunct Nessus *(breaking open)*, and the 6th house is favorably aspected by a conjunction with Venus. 2002 KX14 itself was discovered at the 26th degree of Scorpio in the 10th house, conjunct Scientia and the Plutino of extreme self-control, 2001 KN77, trine Moon in Cancer in the 7th house, and opposite Sun on Algol conjunct Vicia/Klotho/Tezcatlipoca and the Plutinos 1998 US43, 1998 WU31, and 1998 WW24 in the 4th house in Taurus.

In studying various charts, it seems that 2002 KX14 is a powerful force that wants to counter criticism, manage criticism, and purge its own tendency to react to criticism reflexively or self-destructively through absolute principles, turning it into a work force that can plow through like a tank and simply let criticism bounce off its thick skin or calmly and strategically deal with criticism without harming itself. Thus, 2002 KX14 tests self-integrity and the ability to avoid self-harm through reactions to criticism from others. The goal is not to abandon principles, but rather to learn how to defend them both firmly and flexibly, the latter to avoid losing everything since principles are part of one's overall mindset and should not become an obsession or worse, an obsession. This is reminiscent of the Chinese story of the cherry branch and the willow branch. The cherry branch boasts that it is much harder, more inflexible, and stronger than the willow branch. Then, in the autumn, the first snow falls, causing the cherry branch to break under the weight while the willow branch simply bends and springs back. In charts where 2002 KX14 is heavily afflicted or in contact with 2001 KF77, one seems to want to learn this lesson, but rarely manages to sustainably manage the energy of this Cubewano positively.

Since criticism can also be just and nourishing, 2002 KX14 in the elephant hide mode can also create a new problem, namely, becoming desensitized and alienated from reality and one's own activities to the point of making oneself impossible in every way. Politicians are particularly susceptible to this, and it leads in only two directions. Either they fall out of favor and into political decline, or they are embraced by the higher political lobby and lose every shred of self-integrity and authenticity, and with it, any form of self-governance. They then sell their soul to the devil, so to speak.

A heavily afflicted 2002 KX14 has problems with the functioning of the root chakra, which underperforms, and the third chakra, which simultaneously over-functions. It seems as if the Nessus energy in 2002 KX14 is going off the rails in a verbal "rape" campaign while defending against criticism, the official truth, or trying to make a point. This occurs mainly in people with a strong sense of justice and activist idealism. (Rhadamantus is in 8 conjunct cusp 9 in the discovery horoscope of 2002 KX14.) Rhine flint is a good stone to wear, preferably in both pockets, as it restores and harmonizes communication between the root chakra, third chakra, and sixth chakra (command center, self-control, vision).

The orbital period is 242 years and 117 days.

145452 2005 RN43

Paranormal research; problems with livelihood and ones love life.

2005 RN43 was discovered on September 10th, 2005 by A.C. Becker, A.W. Puckett and J.M. Kubica and has a diameter of 679 km.

If prominently aspected, 2005 RN43 emanates a predominantly negative influence that stifles and hinders life and future prospects. This Cubewano is only suitable for thorough paranormal research, but it remains difficult to obtain sufficient resources unless one can carry out research at a subsidized institution or similar. In the past, this object would have offered more opportunities than currently. Characteristics include: deep interest in paranormal matters; parapsychology; structural parapsychological research; suicidal thoughts or tendencies due to the loss of resources, supplies, or something that has been built up with great care; and difficult or poor love and relationship life.

The famous critical researcher and author of books on paranormal phenomena (poltergeists, séances), Harry Price, had 2005 RN43 in the 10th degree of Virgo conjunct Aten *(wanting to communicate something)*; opposite Venus and trine Neptune. Price was very popular (Venus) with a large audience, which provided him with a lot of help in investigating cases, and was appreciated for his objective scientific and unbiased approach. Paranormal researcher Renée Aynes described him as one of the most fascinating and storm-provoking figures in psychical research.

The orbital period is 265 years and 362 days.

202421 2005 UQ513 (NAME SUGGESTION: HELLE)

Burglaries or preventing burglaries; violent conflicts between life partners; a very violent death; one partner killing the other; wanting to expand and grow through relationships, contracts or diplomacy; prolonged antagonism; prolonged anxiety; obsession; compulsiveness; energy release; anticipation of severe deterioration and post-traumatic stress disorder.

Cubewano and dwarf planet candidate, discovered on October 21, 2005 by Michael E. Brown, David L. Rabinowitz, and Chad Trujillo with a diameter of approximately 498 km. The Minor Planet Center classified this object as a Cubewano, but the Deep Ecliptic Survey noted 2005 UQ513 as a Scattered Disc Object.

2005 UQ513 has a predominantly dark energy with a playing field mainly in the space between two partners. Characteristics include: home invasions or the prevention of break-ins; intense conflicts between partners arising from miscommunication or arrogance of one partner in relation to their social status (specifically conflicts between an academically educated partner and one without that academic education); a very violent death; one partner killing the other; a desire to expand and grow through relationships, contracts, or diplomacy.

Astrologer Francesco Schiavinotto links 2005 UQ513 to long-term obstruction, long-term anxiety, obsession, compulsiveness, the release of energy, anticipation of serious deterioration, and post-traumatic stress disorder. The sign and house and the aspecting can provide a very precise and explicit description of the essence and cause of one's obsession, chronic anxiety, or accumulated stress disorder or PTSS.

2005 UQ513 can inflict heavy wounds. Yet, in a positive sense and related to the sudden release of a lot of energy, 2005 UQ513 can also help to overcome severe trauma and let go of things like resentment and other emotional obsessive ties. This Cubewano challenges the strongest among the strong and is further suitable for therapeutic assistance in trauma, obsessions, anxiety disorders, and burnout. One must always guard against obsession and a strong understanding of what obsession and an obsessive person are must be developed.

In this latter respect lies the only treasure buried by 2005 UQ513, namely becoming free from obsessors, which is about the greatest challenge for all of humanity because without this freedom from obsessors and obsessions, a sustainable state of freedom will never be achieved.

I suggest the name Helle, after the Norse goddess of the underworld. Obsessions are the building blocks and essence of hell, for everyone personally, embedded with various commonalities in the zeitgeist.

The orbital period is 283 years and 347 days.

307261 2002 MS4

Superconsciousness; tender and responsible towards the other in creation; context-sensitive; karmic insight; causal and acausal cause-effect insight; being able to masterfully combine diverse complexities and seemingly contradictory elements into a workable organon; the breakthrough of a group consciousness.

2002 MS4 was discovered on June 18, 2002 by Michael E. Brown and Chad Trujillo. It is a large object, possibly a dwarf planet, with a diameter of 808 km, making it, at the time of this writing, one of the ten largest TNOs.

2002 MS4 operates as a kind of universal higher self, with extreme sensitivity and superb awareness of the consequences of every action. This consciousness extends far beyond death, zeitgeist, and the incarnations of entire generations. For this reason, 2002 MS4 is astrologically associated with ongoing feedback loops, a thorough spiritual awareness, and a striving for spiritual certainty. When talking about sensitivity and superb awareness of the consequences of every action, of course, there should be a benchmark or frame of reference. This framework is humanity itself, meaning what makes humans humane, tender, and responsible towards others in creation.

Key concepts: spiritual orientation; super-insight; superb awareness; higher-self contact and guidance; context sensitivity; karmic awareness; karmic insight; the breakthrough of a group consciousness; causal and acausal cause-effect insight; the masterful combination of various complexities and seemingly conflicting elements into a workable organon. In a negative sense, these 2002 MS4 qualities can go completely over the top. Various bodies such as Neptune, Tara, Salacia, Sila-Nunam, Venus, 2004 EW95, and for example, 1999 TC36 can increase the sensitivity and perceptual abilities of 2002 MS4 to such an extent that the planet is essentially paralyzed, because there are too many trees to see the forest of the organon. 2002 MS4 only comes alive if enough other energies are linked to it to make concrete, convincing, and executable translations, for example, through science or philosophy, art, a spiritual framework, or therapy.

The orbital period is 269 years and 175 days.

471921 2013 FC 28
Resisting evil with creativity; being felled by negative superpowers; nirguna, vajrayana.

2013 FC 28 is a small celestial object that measures approximately 420 to 446 km in diameter and was discovered twice. The latest discovery was made on March 17th, 2013 by Scott S. Sheppard and Chad A. Trujillo, while the first discovery dates back to March 21st, 1999 in the 8th degree of Virgo, conjunct Logos trine 2002 VE93/2005 RR43 and conjunct Thuban (alpha Draco), a star that used to serve as a Pole Star before being replaced by Polaris. In astrological terms, Thuban is associated with trading, managing or administering gold and silver neutrally, and negative events related to the Fire-element, such as the loss of a house due to fire. The Sun at the time of discovery was conjunct with 2003 WL7/1994 TB/1996 TO66/Sethos, sextile 1988 XB in Aquarius, and square Nessus in Capricorn. The Moon was in Taurus, Venus in Taurus square Neptune/Photographia, and Mercury conjunct Mors-Somnus.

Astrologically, 2013 FC28 represents the ability to refrain from responding aggressively or irritably to external negativity, thus protecting oneself from becoming obsessed or infiltrated by what one despises, and being derailed by it. However, this is a challenging Cubewano to handle, as it often involves collusive injustice (corruption by government or large organizations) that is difficult to penetrate administratively, bureaucratically, or legally. The key is to maintain a connection with one's self-integrity and passionate drive to overcome the resulting spiritual darkness (Mercury conjunct Mors-Somnus) by finding or regaining nourishment from the good things in life.

One of the biggest temptations to resist is seeking refuge in alcohol or drug use. 2013 FC28 requires a high level of individual capability and will result in tragedy and loss 9 times out of 10, but one time out of 10 will produce a hero in the truest sense of the word. The celestial object is strongly associated with nirguna (Kali's touch), the collapse of all mindsets for a rebirth from one's own strength, which is a state of fearlessness achieved through a profound identification aka fusion of ones self with atman.

The underlying driving force behind 2013 FC 28 is realizing a positive Leo identity after purging the negative aspects of Scorpio and Libra to attain integrity and balance. Ultimately, the fruit of this process is a warm personality that exudes courage, earned authority, and virtually untouchable integrity.

The object has an orbital period of 314 years and 7 days.

Ignis.

Hioltzius excudebat. A° 1586.

...ea conuexi vis, et sine pondere coelum   Emicuit, summaq́ locum sibi legit in arce

HAUMEIDS

136108 HAUMEA

The first sprout that will fill a void; Shakti's essence; regeneration; Mother Earth; women's rights; fertility; rebirthing; preservation of youthful energy, regeneration; focal point of growth; nurturing energy; bringing forth; generating different things or legacies that will lead their own lives; correlational dialectical synergy, replacing cyclic dualism with thinking in complementary forces; the issue of abortion

Haumea is an "ex-Cubewano", which means that this recognized dwarf planet and Pluto-like object is now considered part of a separate family, the *Haumea family* or *Haumeids*. Haumea was discovered on December 28, 2004 by Michael E. Brown, Chadwick Trujillo, and David Lincoln Rabinowitz, and is named after the Hawaiian goddess of childbirth. In July 2005, the discovery of Haumea was again claimed by another research team that was unaware of the earlier discovery. This Spanish team consisted of J. L. Ortiz, F. J. Aceituno, and P. Santos Sanz.

The first discovery team suggested the name Ataecina for Haumea. Ataecina or Ataegina was the ancient Celtic-Iberian goddess of rebirth. That name comes from atte and geno (reborn). Haumea has a rugby ball-shaped body measuring $2100 \times 1680 \times 1074$ km, with two small moons, Hi'iaka and Namaka, orbiting around it.

In Hawaiian mythology, Haumea is a significant goddess and, just like the Celtic-Iberian Ataecina, associated with fertility, childbirth, and motherhood. She is revered as a powerful and nurturing deity who plays a crucial role in the cycle of life and creation. Haumea is often depicted as a motherly figure, symbolizing the abundance and productivity of the land. She is closely connected to the natural world, embodying the life-giving forces of the earth. Haumea is particularly associated with the growth and sustenance of plants, crops, and the overall fertility of the land. In Hawaiian folklore, Haumea is considered the mother of the Hawaiian islands. Legend has it that she gave birth to the islands and their various features, such as mountains, valleys, and rivers. This symbolic association reflects her role as a creator and life-giver.

Haumea is also known for her transformative abilities. In some stories, she has the power to shape-shift and change her form, representing the ever-changing nature of life and the cycles of birth, growth, and renewal. This aspect of her mythology highlights her adaptability and resilience. As a revered goddess, Haumea is honored through prayers, rituals, and ceremonies. People seek her blessings for fertility, successful pregnancies, and the prosperity of their land and crops. She is considered a guardian and protector of the natural world, reminding people of their connection to the earth and the importance of sustainable practices.

Taking into account our current zeitgeist, Haumea appears to serve as the counterpart to Makemake within a process where the living, feminine, and natural contrast with the advancing artificial focused on blind peak performance, digitalization, and integration with machines, thus positioning nature and Mother Earth in opposition to the technosphere.

The astrological interpretation suggests: The divine; the first germ of growth that will fill a vacuum of being; the essence of Shakti; fertility; rebirthing; preservation of youthful energy, regeneration; growth point; nurturing energy; producing different things or leaving behind things that will lead their own lives; cherishing, protecting and promoting what is natural and countering what is unnatural; understanding that natural creation is not only a reference frame for humans, but also part of their soul that keeps them human – and also understanding that the dwindling of nature due to the overriding of technology, electrification, digitization, industrialization, transhumanism, and administration will be its downfall; anti-modernism; anti-digitization; anti-Big Brother; cyclical consciousness; ecology; earth and human-friendly solutions to problems; understanding the essence of life; replacing dualism with distinguishing complementary forces that must be in synergy; lively insight; problem-solving; mentally alert; aware of threats; life-shocking events. Forensics: striving for peace; pantheism; pursuing a dynamic yin-yang synergy; nature religion; the Great Mother; original witch cults; being rooted; root chakra and sacral chakra.

The house, sign, and aspecting and degree position provide a lot of additional information regarding Haumea in the natal chart, it reveals how and with what one can recharge, recover, recuperate, or emotionally, mentally, or spiritually regenerate. When in contact with Uranus, Haumea has a mundane connection with women's rights and abortion issues, as well as resistance to male, religious, or state oppression of women in general.

Haumea's orbital period is 283 years and 44 days.

416400 2003 UZ117

Crisis management; elimination or absence of emotions or uncertain or deformed expression of feelings; sense of being lost, cursed or unpleasantly connected to cosmic energy; keen antennae for threats that no one notices, but usually turn out to be correct; trouble shooting; cleanup work; thankless work; remediating organizations; great decisiveness; decisions with impact; executions, foreclosure sales; bankruptcy counseling.

2003 UZ117 was discovered by Spacewatch on October 24, 2003 and is estimated to be 138 to possibly 423 km in diameter. This Haumea-like object is suitable for work and actions that require persistence and where emotions or sentiments have to be shut down in order to get the job done.

Characteristics: earthly, thorough, and purposeful; expresses itself mainly through consultation, meeting, human resource work, and reporting; heavy, plutonic, sometimes dark or magical charisma; confrontational; pushing or thrusting; cutting the knot; cold rationality; lonely, even in company; suppression or absence of emotions or uncertain or deformed emotional expression; feeling of loss, curse, or unpleasant connection with cosmic energy; sharp sensitivity to threats that no one notices, but usually turn out to be true; cool and authoritative, but sometimes with suppressed anger; mentally sharp, original and out of the box; sober visionary; opening Pandora's box out of necessity in a well-founded way; concentrated; a solitary management position or someone who works alone; goal-oriented, but may take a long time to achieve the goal; endurance; long-term ambitions; crisis management; trouble shooting; cleanup work; thankless work; organizational restructuring; great decision-making power; decisions with impact; executions; foreclosures; bankruptcy guidance; strategic use or abuse of NLP; gallows humor; calculated, thoroughly considered suicide or advice to others to prevent it; black magic; complex, difficult to fathom or gauge mind.

Forensic: someone who is not very popular but necessary to get the job done; government advisers; reorganizations; bankruptcies.

The orbital period is 292 years and 139 days.

308193 2005 CB79

Schizoid, successful Frankenstein technology; high-tech that deprives the individual of personal freedom or fails to respect personal boundaries; a huge gap between love and real connecting, sham connections; a mix of useful success and empty success, which has to rely only on image and trend boosting; technical talent coupled with abundance; the challenge as well as the failure to integrate technology with human rights, respect for environment and health requirements.

2005 CB79 was discovered on February 6, 2005 by Michael E. Brown, Chadwick Trujillo, and David Lincoln Rabinowitz and measures 158 km in diameter. Its meaning points to a logical mind. Aptitude for exact sciences and computer science is linked to success in the fields of work, career, and finances, as well as the option to open a door to something very harmful and negative. Someone with 2005 CB79 in a very strong position can become rich and successful, with the caveat that their work has a side that cannot withstand scrutiny.

Ex-nazi scientist Herman P. Schwan (brought to the USA via Operation Paperclip) – the inventor of the longest lasting, most universally used piece of fake science that cloaks the severe heath effects of microwaves with a nonsense formula, known as SAR (measures health effect solely in terms of thermal effects) – had 2005 CB79 conjunct the fame-Centaur Bienor in 24 Sagittarius.

Steve Jobs had 2005 CB79 in 15 Gemini, among others conjunct Victoria/ Scientia *(scientific breakthrough)*; trine Mercury in 15 Aquarius *(pushing the boundaries of communication)*; trine Swift in Libra *(able to make quick contact)*; inconjunct Chariklo/Manwë-Thorondor/Siegena/2002 VR128 *(successful futurological propaganda packaged in an almost spiritual aura)*; semi-sextile Hylonome/Charybdis *(engulfing popularity)*. He is the prototype for this Haumeidian. He was and is revered by many as a kind of messiah, while his company, Apple, has behaved so horrible with regard to human rights, child labor, working conditions, and environmental pollution that a whole documentary was made about it. His iPad – leaning 100% on the fake-science of Schwan – may cause hundreds of thousands of children and young adults to die prematurely from cancer or leukemia in the near future due to the insane levels of radiation these devices emit, which is ridiculously higher than what is considered building biology-safe. This is apart from harmful effects on children's brain development, infolepsis (pathological addiction to digital information), and early onset dementia development (see the work of brain authority Dr. Manfred Spitzer). Jobs' entire work is based on the increasingly eroding lies spread by health councils and the WHO regarding the real risks of Wi-Fi and high-frequency radiation. (Over 10.000 scientific studies have already been published on this subject, which are being covered up.)

2005 CB79 also rules over high-tech that deprives the individual of personal freedom or does not respect personal boundaries. There is a great gap in love and real connection with this Haumeidian. Only apparent connection seems to result from it. Because technical talent is directly linked to abundance and "success," the path to healing in this area is far-fetched, though not impossible.

The link with the spiritual dimension is actually destroyed in 2005 CB79, under the influence of Damocles in the discovery horoscope of 2005 CB79. A dominant 2005 CB79 may interfere with the heart and sacral chakra, deforming the functioning of the root chakra. Most technical problems and misery arise only because products are launched too early with dollar signs in mind. To continue with the Jobs example: the concept of a tablet on which one wirelessly consumes information is, of course, not bad in itself. It is the implementation and choice of microwaves as a carrier that is the pestilence here. Apple computers are excellent devices. It is unfortunate that the mix of useful and harmful will usually win over just the useful. The great challenge of 2005 CB79, therefore, lies in the integration of technology and computer applications with humane standards, human rights, health requirements, environmental requirements, etc. Working in a very harmonious environment is beneficial for this Haumeidian to bring the latter to the fore more easily.

The orbital period is 288 years and 138 days.

145453 2005 RR43

Bridging the gap between passion and career; a strong dissonance between an urge to mean something in public life and one's personal, private passions and interests; LGBT-rights activism; erotic photography; that aspect of the technical that forms the interface between human and technical or digital reality; finding new dimensions; rebooting.

2005 RR43 was discovered on September 9, 2005, by Andrew C. Becke, Andrew Wayne Puckett, and Jeremy M. Kubica and measures approximately 252 km in diameter, although estimates vary.

2005 RR43 is a complex Haumean because it exhibits a strong dissonance between a drive to make an impact in public life and personal, private passions and interests. The work itself and relationships also struggle to come to fruition, but this is mostly because the distant horizon beckons and distracts. Nevertheless, there is great concentration and a capacity for persistence and rebooting. If 2005 RR43 is located in a strong position, such as conjunct Sun, Moon, midheaven, ascendant, or ruler, one must usually reconcile oneself to the fact that there will be a great divide between work/career and the satisfaction one derives from one's own affinities, aspirations, and interests. The problem is that the drive for career success is strong and work remains necessary for livelihood, but the greatest passion and drive manifest outside of work, at the hobby level or in outdoor activities. This is not a rare situation, but a strong 2005 RR43 makes it very explicit. It is also possible that the status or code of behavior associated with work and/or career frustrates one's own passion, needs, and self-integrity.

2005 RR43 is linked to homosexuality and an interest in erotic photography. Furthermore, it indicates technical aptitude, particularly in computer science, and has an affinity with paranormal perception or sensitivity, which is strongly denied or rejected. By being too conventional, the energy of 2005 RR43 can be very much in the way. It seems that the best advice for someone with a dominant 2005 RR43 is to try to make their hobby their work, thereby allowing the IC to determine the direction more than the midheaven. Francesco Schiavinotto associates 2005 RR43 with leadership, the commander, someone who can influence human behavior and find new dimensions.

Russian LGBT-rights activist Nikolay Alexandrovich Alexeyev had 2005 RR43 prominently placed: conjunct Yes; square Black Moon; square Mercury; conjunct Midpoint Black Moon/Mercury; opposite Orcus. American LGBT-rights and human rights activist Elisabeth Birch had conjunct uncorrected Black Moon/Sethos/2001 UR163/1998 WU31; trine Varda; square 1999 OY3; square 2003 WL7. Elmer Batters, a German pioneer in fetish photography, had 2005 RR43 conjunct 1993 SB *(image obsession)*; sextile Uranus/2005 UJ438 *(highly sensitive to the exceptional)*; square Eris/Ceto; conjunct midpoint Uranus-Industria. Finally, 2005 RR43 (source: transneptunian.astrology. blogspot) is associated with "the instrument"; interfacing between human and computer.

Its orbital period is 283 years and 212 days.

24835 1995 SM55

Breakthrough or transformation for better or worse; conversion; strong acceptance versus rejection issues.

1995 SM55 was discovered on September 19, 1993 by Nichole Danzl and has a diameter of 174 km, although another estimate puts it at 704 km.

In its core, 1995 SM55 deals with a breakthrough within the integrity of one's own development, creativity, spirituality, individualization process, and thus also with the start of a new phase or completion of what one has been working towards for a long time. The breakthrough can also refer to becoming known to a wider audience. Positively, nurturing breakthroughs include inventions, discoveries, breaking mindsets, and fixed frameworks, etc. Negatively, 1995 SM55 represents a very rough, wild, and aggressive breaking or breaking into something for the sake of publicity, to compensate for inferiority complexes, at any cost and regardless of the means or method.

Charles Manson has 1995 SM55 conjunct North Node/Lugh *(skills)* /2010 EN65 *(detonation)* / Offenbach *(much ado)* / Ilias *(myth-making)* on Midpoint Lilith/Hylonome *(becoming known for child murder)* -Flammario *(occult insight)*; square 1999 TD10 *(invasion)*; square 2003 AZ84 *(penetrating investigation)*. Despite Manson, 1995 SM55 is completely neutral in terms of good or bad and is represented more in positive breakthroughs than negative ones. 1995 SM55 is strongly Uranian, original, out of the box, innovative, and system-breaking (Bruce Lee, Boyan Slat, Rupert Sheldrake, Nikola Tesla). Mark Andrew Holmes associates 1995 SM55 with acceptance and effectiveness issues, rejection, isolation, persecution, and politics. These links fit in with 1995 SM55 if we only observe the discovery chart (Midheaven trine Pallas; opposition to Machiavelli; discovery Moon in 12th trine Nessus/Varda/Thereus; Sun in the 27th degree of Virgo conjunct Siva/Burney trine Uranus in the 27th degree of Capricorn). The Mercurial side of 1995 SM55 has a magical touch (conjunct Deucalion; square Flammario). 1995 SM55 tries to establish the new, original, and breakthrough. Air, the idea, is grounded in the concrete. What breaks through new things always encounters either enthusiasm and admiration or resistance and opposition.

Emotionally, 1995 SM55 is isolated, and strong chart position of this Haumeid is not helpful in terms of love and relationships, except for separations. 1995 SM55 thrives best in a creative environment, a situation where there is a stalemate of heavy, stiff, and cumbersome planets or asteroids, and the need for a piece of blue between the clouds is great. Breakthrough can very well take the form of a conversion of one thing into another. Therefore, 1995 SM55 is also linked to computer simulation (transneptunian.astrology. blogspot). We must not forget that we carry a supercomputer in our own head and body. Therefore, 1995 SM55 also seems to be about interpreting reality or a derivative, such as language to a communication organon. The essence is captured and processed into something else, which can be expressed artistically, for example, in graphic form or braille, or representation via other media, materials, or expressions. Computer simulation may be one of the most perfect possibilities in this direction, but by no means the only option.

The deceased Dutch top psychic Anton Pauwe strangely had 1995 SM55 conjunct Utopia *(vision of the future, utopia)* opposite Haumea, of which 1995 SM55 is one of the fragments (1995 SM55 11°17 Aquarius - opposition Haumea 11°23 Rx Leo). 1995 SM55 was sextile Saturn. The London magician-artist Austin Osman Spare had 1995 SM55 at 8°54 Sagittarius opposite Haumea at 8°42 Rx Gemini. 1995 SM55 was conjunct Siwa *(fertility)* and 2010 EN65 *(detonation, sexual discharge)*. Anton Pauwe repeatedly demonstrated his remote viewing ability live on the radio show "Het Zwarte Gat", by mentally transporting himself to the living room of a caller and describing in detail how the room looked. It was always a very impressive demonstration of remote viewing. However, in this process, a translation occurred from the actual room to an image in Pauwe's brain. Austin Osman Spare is known for his unique magical alphabet and is considered the godfather of chaos magic, in which the orgasm (2010 EN65) is usually used to launch a mental translation of a desired reality into the causal reality, after which this charged thought-form must materialize in the actual reality via the morphogenetic field.

The orbital period is 268 years and 215 days.

386723 2009 YE7

Learn to ground inspiration and creativity; becoming frustrated in recognition; running out of resources, or supplies or money due to unexpected twists and turns or neglect; learning to refrain from a narcissistic Bohemian attitude; preventing one's own creativity from being exploited by others; sticking creatively and professionally to one project until it is finished and only then starting the next one.

2009 YE7 was discovered by David Lincoln Rabinowitz on December 17, 2009, with the discovery position conjunct Algol. Its diameter is estimated to be 570 km, although other estimates vary both up and down. 2009 YE7 crosses the orbits of Pluto and Neptune, but its orbit is more eccentric.

2009 YE7 inspires and gives artistic affinity, making one creative, artistically project-oriented, and best expressed through visual language, such as painting and visual arts. Where 2009 YE7 makes a strong aspect with bodies related to language expression, such as Mercury, Hermes, or the axis of the 3rd and 9th houses, language use is highly visual and imaginary. However, 2009 YE7 gives problems with recognition and a feeling of remaining in the shadows with these activities and not shining as it should – incorrectly. Artistic achievements must go through a process of fighting for recognition, apart from the fact that something of high quality must be produced.

The aspecting and positioning of 2009 YE7 give more clues about how and with what to free this energy, as well as the dos and don'ts. Financially, there may be a certain immorality or lack of principle. There is always a risk of running out of means, supplies, or money due to unexpected turns or neglect of this aspect. 2009 YE7 remains highly inspired. Important for a dominant position of this object is to stand on one's own feet, have self-confidence, beware of inflated pride, stay with creativity, and first establish a strong, respected position before embarking on projects with others, so that they do not take all creative input and the self is pushed out of the nest like a cuckoo, or dismissed with a small amount of "pocket money." Nature works nourishing and healing, as well as contemplating the concepts of contraction and expansion.

The orbital period is 294 years and 288 days.

19308 1996 TO66 (NAME SUGGESTION: UGLY)

The ugly, the provocative, or the vanishing; an audacious challenge to societal, religious, or political norms, aimed at unveiling concealed truths or suppressed necessities; an inherently distorted means of expression, driven to its limits; the unacceptable.

Haumeid and weak 11:19 Neptune-resonant of approximately 409 km in length, discovered on October 12, 1996 by Chadwick Trujillo, David C. Jewitt, and Jane X. Luu.

As I draw a rather divergent conclusion about the functioning of 1996 TO66 than various colleagues researching trans-Neptunian celestial bodies, I substantiate it with more case examples and discovery horoscope data than usual. From his own research, Russian Gennady Maslov concludes that this object is always associated with loss, disappearance, theft, embezzlement, and the realization that nothing lasts forever; in short, he links 1996 TO66 to the awareness of transience and the relativity of possession. Mark Andrew Holmes assigns a completely different interpretation, that of having some kind of vision. John Delaney is somewhere in between: ambitious failures by talented people; revolution from the top, grand ambition; a connection with the spiritually inclined or arising from strong instincts or gut feelings or emotions; challenges on a scale beyond the given capabilities; success through continuity; viewing the future as an extension of existing history.

My own research, in which I conclude that 1996 TO66 is primarily concerned with the ugly, repulsive, and obscene, has some overlap with this. Regarding the discovery horoscope, the Sun of 1996 TO66 is in the 20th degree of Libra (in Via Combusta), conjunct Tezcatlipoca/Asbolus/Chiron/2001 KF77 at the Midpoint Ceres|Orcus opposition Eris/Germania. The Sun is square Verdun/cusp 3 and cusp 9. The discovery Moon is weak in 16 Libra (also in Via Combusta, and 4 degrees before the exact New Moon) conjunct Sauer *(acidic, cranky)* / 2003 FB128 *(continue, push through)*.

Somewhat in contrast to this, 1996 TO66 has a Venus/Dionysus trine Jupiter, with Venus, however, awkwardly positioned in Virgo and Jupiter not optimal in Capricorn. Mercury is in 5 Libra conjunct Amun and Pholus; trine Midheaven; sextile Nessus/Spartacus opposition 1992 QB1/1993 SB/1993 SC/Dong. Mercury is very ambitious, the mind very stimulated, but it is very difficult to give direction to it, while it is as it were hitting its head against the wall with Pholus and Nessus; strengthened by the Sun-2001 KF77 conjunction. The discovery position of 1996 TO66 itself is the 29th degree of Pisces under the influence of the star Scheat, in 5 degrees under 6, where an exact trine is made to Sethos *(curse)* in Cancer and an exact trine to Ixion/Circe/Eros/Cupid/cusp 7 *(bad karma or process mixed with relational and sexual issues or public enemies)*. The discovery ascendant in 28 Taurus is squared by Toro/Requiem/Paranal from Leo *(piety meeting brutality)* and the Centaur Elatus from Aquarius *(chameleon-like assimilation driven by a desire for freedom)*. Randi *(lust)* is on the cusp of 12.

With a strong 1996 TO66, there is a great need for expression, but the ability to express oneself often becomes something explicitly deformed or carries this in a debilitating way. Both the communication axis and the feeling itself and the expression of emotion are problem areas. Often, extremes are sought to feel something or to express feelings, or to make emotional contact, or the feeling is gone. In this respect, sexual extremes seem to be nourishing and relaxing. In a positive sense, 1996 TO66 is a taboo breaker for things that people or society want to sweep under the rug. The ugly, the non-conforming, the unwanted, and what is deemed obscene, have a place in reality and normally humans can override the harmful effect through openness, honesty and emancipation. The Dutch expressionist painter and musician Herman Brood constantly said things that were considered socially unacceptable. But always with a coarse, sympathetic, and disarming form of humor. Brood was at a certain point almost the court jester of the Netherlands, with privileges that no one else was able to acquire ("I have a very special relationship with the tax authorities. I never paid any taxes"). Brood's "ugliness" was further expressed in the way he completely destroyed his body with alcohol and drugs, and he had an intense aversion to ever withering away as an old man behind the geraniums. Brood had 1996 TO66 conjunct Yes/Panthera/1998 WW24; sextile Moon/Amor; sextile Child; square Varuna.

Much of the misery in the world arises from the suppression of natural impulses and needs that are deemed undesirable, after which the energy of these impulses gets twisted in a way that is much more harmful than it needed to be. In the most negative sense, the ugly, dirty, or obscene is expressed in a way that harms others, as is the case with the Dutch prime minister Mark Rutte (1996 TO66 conjunct Sun/Machiavelli/Hylonome), who is personally entangled with the disappearance of over 1000 Dutch children (toeslagen-affaire) and as a youth called for legalization of sex with the under-aged. According to the independent news circuit, he is described as the most immoral, cowardly, and harmful prime minister that the Netherlands has ever had, leaving a trail of destruction, lies, misery, and economic and societal decline, while upgrading the collusive status (institutionalized state corruption) of the Dutch government to an unprecedented level. During his reign, most cartoons and posts about him spread on social media were expressions of intense disgust for him as a person, his party, and his policies. Sometimes, burying the ugly and obscene is a thousand times worse than showing it.

In the chart of the Dutch ex-NOS news chief editor Marcel Gelauff, we see 1996 TO66 in opposition to Uranus; conjunct 2001 UO18 *(assessing relationships)* and square Itokawa *(revealing news)*. The NOS news, funded by the Dutch government, used and uses a totallitarian news censorship, framing, ignoring every rule for decent journalism as internationally agreed upon in the *Bordeaux Code*. However, this happens everywhere in the West.

The German ex-mainstream journalist Udo Ulfkotte, who passed away in 2016, could no longer tolerate this and openly turned against the CIA-infiltrated European press agencies in his books *Journalists for Hire: How the CIA Buys the News*, etc.. He had 1996 TO66 in 17 Aquarius sextile Typhon *(fighting or struggling)*. We see a similar journalistic turn in Micha Kat, a former *Telegraaf* mainstream journalist, who also had 1996 TO66 sextile Typhon, and turned against the mainstream journalistic cover-up of the pedophile network.

In film director David Lynch, we see a very different expression of the ugly and obscene through the *Twin Peaks* series and his character Laura Palmer – a beloved girl who was murdered – and who later became involved with a dark demonic group of young people, linked to sex and violence, led by an evil entity named Bob. Lynch has 1996 TO66 conjunct Venus *(love)*.

Philosopher of the "evil and obscene" Georges Bataille, who wrote explicitly obscene erotica and philosophized against the repression of such impulses, had 1996 TO66 conjunct Amor *(conquering or wanting to score in love)*; square Randi *(lust)* and square Chaos *(chaos and originality)*, also on the Midpoint of Randi/Chaos.

Annie Sprinkle, who from an otherwise positive post-hippie motivation made a business of publicly masturbating in front of an audience, has 1996 TO66 square Moon; trine Enterprise *(entrepreneurship)*; sextile Eris/Orius *(fighting for hippie ideals)*. Sprinkle believed that her orgasms contributed to healing the world.

Leopold Sacher-Masoch, author of *Venus in Furs* from which the
term sadomasochism was derived, had 1996 TO66 in 12 Leo opposite
Ascendant/2001 FL194; conjunct cusp 7 *(relationships)* on the Midpoint
formed by two trines Pandora|Yeti|Villon – Amor.

The brilliant creator and producer of the *Breaking Bad* and *Better Call Saul*
series, Vince Gilligan, has 1996 TO66 strongly aspected, including – very
fascinatingly – conjunct Hermes/2002 VE95 *(clever mix of creativity and
drugs)*. *Breaking Bad* revolves entirely around the production of crystal meth.
Hermes' devilish humor also manifests in *Better Call Saul* in aspect with 1996
TO66 as the character Jimmy/Saul uses floaters in the toilet to get fired from a
law firm. He was also once convicted for defecating through the open roof of
his ex-girlfriend's friend's car, but did not notice that there were still children
in the car.

Hotkinkyo crosses the line for many seasoned porn enthusiasts by performing
the most extreme acts with her anus. In her chart, 1996 TO66 is conjunct her
17-degree Pisces sex degree and trine Saturn/Arawn in Scorpio.

Mike Rowe, the host of the successful Discovery series *Dirty Jobs* – who
himself performs dirty work in every episode – has 1996 TO66 sextile Typhon/
Hilda *(fighting into something dark)*, square Toro *(ad hoc concretization)*, and
conjunct 2001 BL41 *(abundance)*.

Peter Acworth, CEO of kink.com, which became the largest porn company
in the world, and who became known for hogtied.com and fuckingmachines.
com, where women undergo very extreme machine-driven orgasms, has
1996 TO66 trine Quaoar *(extensive development and growth structure)* in
the first degree Scorpio, from the last degree of Aquarius *(putting everything
into crossing or shifting boundaries)*. Furthermore, 1996 TO66 opposes Lilith/
Dionysus/BAM; square Atropos/Tantalus in Sagittarius. Tantalus *(torture)*
refers to the intensity of the sex, which is so great that his models often have to
take breaks.

The combination of 1996 TO66 with Poutanen *(prostituting)* is present in
various porn stars. Jan Wolkers, who was groundbreaking in the Netherlands
as a writer on taboos surrounding typical 1996 TO66 matters and who made
paintings of cow shit, had 1996 TO66 conjunct Juno/Serendip/1994 TB;
square the creative 5th house - 11th house axis; square Typhon/Echeclus/2005
UJ438. This Haumea can also make a significant impact during transits.

During her pee-sex scandal, in which a video was leaked showing the Dutch singer Patricia Paay letting herself being urinated upon, she had 1996 TO66 transiting her natal Sun.

I believe that 1996 TO66 is a heavyweight, with everything revolving around how we deal with the dark side of the mind, the ugly, the unaccepted. I also believe that extremes or things that are labeled as extreme by consensus in the realm of sex or drugs are often a release for stress or an emotional gap – or wound – and that normal communication fails. This does not mean that there is no room for change and development in this area.

Other characteristics of 1996 TO66, both personal and forensic: bad luck, unfortunate circumstances, oppressive darkness, or work involving soot, dirt, or poison, or obscure practices, tactics, or concepts; SM, bondage, masochism, femme fatale, cursed loves and relationships; self-undoing by dangerous moves on the communication axis 3rd house - 9th house; bizarre, sick, or dark ambitions and aspirations; seedy scenes; escaping into alcohol or drugs; horror movies; special effects and makeup talent for horror movies; frustrated ideals; declining businesses; sewers, coal mines, mine accidents, engineering in the field of mines or sewers or solving pollution problems; waste disposal, garbage collectors, water pollution – Boyan Slat who invented a device to fish plastic waste out of the sea has 1996 TO66 conjunct Discovery *(discovery)*; square Galactica Center *(technology)*; trine Ixion *(complex creations and processes and negative karma, as involved here in a machine that cleans up what humans dumped in the ocean)* – relevant plastic surgery; coal dust; toxic fallout; genealogy; sexually dominated by the 11th and 12th houses; wanting to be dominated; sex and pain combinations; sexual extremes; fucking machines; BDSM; experiencing one's own core as a threat and source of suffering and misfortune; the obscene, pestilent, or contaminating, pornographically shocking, excrement; the rectum; sadism; political or industrial affairs and deeds that cannot withstand the light of day; cruelty; atrocities to relieve one's own wound pain; whistleblowers; whistleblowers who come to a bad end; porn stars, especially the more extreme ones; neo-Nazis. The suggestion of "Ugly" as a name will no longer require explanation.

The orbital period is 283 years and 190 days.

120178 2003 OP32 (NAME SUGGESTION: LEONARD)

The visionary dissenter; validate the unconventional perspective; boldly challenge the status quo while remaining resilient; face misjudgment from others; edgy in questioning established ethics, the notion of "normalcy," and spirituality; adept at provoking others to make pivotal choices; possess a talent for Neuro-Linguistic Programming (NLP); embody visionary qualities; adept at distilling vast amounts of complex information and perceptions into accessible concepts; possess a commanding presence with profound mystical charisma; a captivating orator; unwaveringly truthful in matters of spirituality.

2003 OP23 was discovered on July 26, 2003, by Michael E. Brown, Chadwick Trujillo, and David Lincoln Rabinowitz, and the diameter is given as either 230 km or 666 km.

Like 2003 OP23, 2003 OP32 exhibits the complexity and broad energetic scope that is characteristic of Haumeids in general. Conjunction with the Sun, Ruler, Midheaven, or Ascendant can result in a powerful spiritual, mystical, religious, philosophical, or magical personality. The type of cult leader, prophet, disseminator of a comprehensive new vision, religious, political or occult reformer, spiritual leader, or catalyst. Overlapping themes with 2003 OP23 include sensitivity to the times and reflection on time. Often there is a vision of the end and beginning of an era. Other keywords and concepts include colliding with the status quo but being formidable at it; being misjudged by others; edgy regarding existing views on ethics, norms, and spirituality; challenging others to make a man-or-mouse decision; NLP; being visionary; being able to reduce large amounts of complex information and perceptions to transferable handles; having a powerful personality with a lot of mystical charisma; being a powerful speaker; being spiritually integral or not. In a positive sense, it is innovative within the aforementioned context. In a negative sense, one's own self-assurance can turn into a few blinders, losing the ability to handle or trust one's own perception and observation. The ability to adopt the vajrayana state, i.e. uncompromising self-integrity, is crucial for the fruitful and positive use of this energy, as otherwise, there will be a derailment and deformation via the display of attention guru behavior. Furthermore, the new philosophy and spiritual conception must be connected to the Earth, the divine, living, and natural. Discovery Vertex conjunct Diana/Haumea). The great blind spot and wound of the zeitgeist are the stepping stone for growth and expansion.

I suggest the name Leonard for this Haumea descendant because the sign Leo is very strong in the discovery horoscope, and Leonard was a nickname for the leader/horned spirit of the medieval witch's Sabbath, in which the original witch cult operated in deep respect and symbiosis with Mother Earth. (Diana/ Haumea conjunct Vertex *(destiny)* in the discovery horoscope). The positive energy of 2003 OP23 is masculine but aimed at restoring the divine feminine. The negative energy is reversed, extremely malignant, and only causes havoc up to and including military crimes. The expression of 2003 OP23 in a neutral sense is mainly oral and written. 2003 OP23 will only be properly expressed in a relatively rare number of horoscopes that are nourishing and stimulating to this particular energy from the rest of their horoscope. In a weak horoscope, it will lead to self-aggrandizement or delusions that will be expressed in a spiritual, flighty, and patronizing manner. Witness the multitude of social media gurus, perpetually missing the mark and merely muddling outdated spiritual click bate with superficial and vague statements.

The orbital period is 282 years and 172 days.

55636 2002 TX300 (NAME SUGGESTION: PIMP)

Direct, blunt, criminal, unrefined; mistaking a blunt cocoon vision for universal truth; raw, self-centered, self-absorbed, callous, lacking empathy or respect; harboring a destructive mindset; lacking vision and empathy; persistently avoiding self-reflection; seeking attention through intrusive behavior, desiring recognition from all; demonstrating resilience, suited for demanding tasks requiring perseverance; vulnerable through openness and directness.

2002 TX300 was discovered by the Near-Earth Asteroid Tracking (NEAT) program on October 15, 2002 and measures 143 km in diameter, while another measure gives 320 km.

Strong and personal aspects in the birth chart of 2002 TX300 can result in two types of person, depending on the *Gestalt* of the chart. The first type is an unimaginable boor, coarse, uncouth, holding a blunt tunnel vision for universal truth, rough, selfish, narcissistic, cruel, insensitive, disrespectful, with a "burn Rome after me" mentality, lacking vision, with zero empathy, a chronic fear of self-confrontation, responding weakly when put under pressure, and being Aries-like in the most incorrect way. This type is interested in making themselves as big and impressive as possible by having a big mouth, being loud, present, intrusive, and wanting everyone to know them. In short, there is an exellent predisposition to end up as a pimp, criminal, supervisor, bailiff, mafia boss, greedy manager, greedy banker, or environmental destroyer - specifically through pollution from mining or waste dumping. However, 2002

TX300 has a built-in escape route to become a wrestler, butcher, stonecutter, or sculptor if there is enough counter-force in the horoscope that can give it a lighter, creative, human friendly and artistic destination.

With 2002 TX300, there can be a strong inclination towards drug and alcohol use, with an emphasis on cocaine and strong liquor. 2002 TX300 has a political facet, which will mainly manifest itself as manipulations or regional political scheming in the case of the primitive type. PNAC politician and former wrestler Donald Rumsfeld, for example, had 2002 TX300 conjunct the ascendant (24 Sagittarius)/RISE/midpoint Toro-Burney; trine Jupiter in Leo; trine Uranus/Nessus in Aries; square Echeclus; sextile Altjira.

In the case of the second type, 2002 TX300 will be useful for addressing unacceptable rude behavior (for example, Alex Jones of whistleblower site infowars.com has 2002 TX300 trine Saturn and trine Uranus). Positive 2002 TX300 can also be useful within the realm of tunnel construction, mining, rescue teams working in earthquake zones, metalworkers, and the aforementioned professions of stonecutter, sculptor, and wrestler. In strong aspect with some of the darker Plutinos, 2002 TX300 can play a decisive role in the formation of a psychopathic personality disorder.

There is something about 2002 TX300 that makes interpreting the radix horoscope somewhat more complex. The Haumeids descendant also indicates how one can make oneself very vulnerable within a social context unintentionally via rudeness, i.e., a direct and raw impulse. One shows an Achilles' heel in an unvarnished directness, which can be targeted by others. 2002 TX300 exhibits a calculated nature in a plebeian manner, yet within this façade, it fumbles numerous opportunities due to its primitive and impulsive directness. 2002 TX300 reacts strongly to the specific zodiac degree. Every human being has a facet in which they come across as rude to others or react rudely to a particular item. The degree information, as well as sign, house, and aspecting, provide clarity. I suggest the name Pimp for reasons that will be clear.

The orbital period is 283 years and 44 days.

86047 1999 OY3

Relationship issues; interest in the connections between people, who is in contact with whom; how a relationship becomes a source of freedom and growth instead of sacrificing or hindering one's own individuation process; artistic talent or affinity for the world of art, dreams, mythology; a glamorous allure that possesses an ethereal quality.

1999 OY3 was discovered on July 18, 1999 by Mauna Kea Observatories (MKO) and measures 192 km in diameter.

1999 OY3 is related to issues of relationships and partnership. Specifically, it focuses on how a relationship can become a source of freedom and growth rather than sacrificing or slowing down one's own individuation process. To achieve this, necessary crises must be overcome. 1999 OY3 enhances the ability to articulate problems and conflicts within this realm, but can also cause issues by expressing them in a forceful and absolutist manner. However, there is a very high sensitivity in this area, which usually prevents this from happening. 1999 OY3 provides a predominantly positive, stimulating, and refreshing impulse to relational matters and is beneficial for combining relationships and careers. Additionally, 1999 OY3 indicates artistic ability or affinity for the world of art, dreams, and mythology. With strong aspects, it can give a certain glamorous allure that retains an ethereal quality.

This Haumean object will do more good than harm. The only serious obstacle may be when one's partner becomes a psychologist or relationship therapist and becomes too pushy in trying to understand the issues their partner is dealing with at the time. On the other hand, with strong affliction, especially with a hard Saturn aspect, the partner can seriously hinder or suffocate their own freedom. This is especially true if the partner is averse to, or has blunt judgments about, art, artistic ambitions, or desires for the partner to meet certain external or formal requirements. However, this always applies to a partner who is struggling with their own inability to express themselves and therefore puts a damper on their counterpart's expression.

The orbital period is 288 years and 351 days.

Isbrantsen
Inuentor

C Bean Schilpten

TNOs WITH DEVIANT NEPTUNE RESONANCES

385446 MANWË-THORONDOR

PR, propaganda, advertising, information management, mental agility and flexibility; media manipulations or exposing and addressing them; spin doctors; infowars; the peddling of things, digital snake oil.

Manwë (formally Manwë-Thorondor) was initially classified as a Cubewano, but is now classified as a binary 4:7 Neptune-resonant. Manwë is approximately 150 km in diameter, and Thorondor is estimated to be 108 km. Both objects orbit around a barycenter in about 110 days, at a distance of 6674 km from each other. Manwë (2003 QW111) was discovered by Marc William Buie on August 25, 2003. The discovery of Thorondor followed on July 25, 2006.

Manwë is named after the fictional king of the Valar in J. R. R. Tolkien's Middle-earth Legendarium. Manwë is the chief god and rules over the sky and wind. Thorondor is the Lord of Eagles in the First Age in Tolkien's work. The connection with Tolkien's mythology associates Manwë-Thorondor with air and therefore with spirit, communication, and thinking. This is supported by the discovery horoscopes of both objects, where the Mercury energy in Manwë is catalyzed by the conjunction of Mercury in the 26th degree of Virgo with Chariklo *(future orientation)*; trine Okyrhoe *(acceleration)*; trine Elektra *(electrifying)*. Mercury in the discovery horoscope of Thorondor is in Cancer, conjunct Okyrhoe/Minerva/2003 AZ84 *(deepened understanding)*; trine Torricelli *(weather, whirlwinds)*. Therefore, Philip Sedgwick is correct in his predominantly Mercurial associations of Manwë with the communicative, the quick-witted, but also with public relations, spinning, hype, propaganda, software updates, and avoiding the emotional side of reality: verbally manipulative, obsessed with logic, and making a point rather than addressing the emotionality of situations. This is underscored by the positions of the Sun and Venus in Virgo in the discovery horoscope of Manwë, but less so by the discovery horoscope of Thorondor.

Both Manwë and Thorondor were discovered in Pisces. Manwë is more Virgo-like and Thorondor more Leo-like. A special common denominator is that both objects have the corrected North Node conjunct Bateman. Manwë has this conjunction in Taurus and Thorondor has it in Pisces. The Sun-Venus conjunction in Manwë corresponds to the Leo-like nature of Thorondor. With Manwë-Thorondor, we can be sure of an amplified Mercury energy, a strong influence of the Virgo-Pisces axis, and the Venus/Sun-Leo energy *(the desire to be the center)*. Bateman, the sociopath among the asteroids, obscures the logical outcome of the main function of Manwë-Thorondor – PR, the promotion of something, advertising, spinning of individuals, with a double agenda towards immoral propaganda, manipulation, peddling of things, and digital wind trading. Underlining the Manwë-Thorondor team's aptitude for this field, i.e., campaigning for politicians, health insurers, and large parties in general, are the trine Pallas *(politics)* Jupiter in Manwë and Pallas trine 1998 BU48 *(cash flow)*, assisted by the Pallas trine Rockefellia *(money, popularity)* in Thorondor.

For each object, including binary objects, there is a downside to the coin. Therefore, someone with a dominant Manwë-Thorondor can also be someone who looks right through all propaganda, PR, and media manipulations and is highly likely to do something about it. If asteroid Itokawa and other critical notes strongly appear in the total horoscope, Manwë-Thorondor can also produce an excellent investigative journalist or cultural critic. The infowars, the battle between official information and independent information, which roughly coincided with the acceleration of the internet and the lies after 9/11, is a typical Manwë-Thorondor versus Manwë-Thorondor affair. Manwë-Thorondor always has something to report and wants it quickly. The playing field within which this happens is in second place. In exceptional cases, a very positive Manwë-Thorondor in a humane horoscope is deeply involved in expelling obsessions, entities, and negativity (Sun/Beowulf conjunction in Manwë), opposite the negative Manwë-Thorondor, which wants to implant information.

The orbital period is 289 years and 116 days.

UNNAMED NEPTUNE RESONANTS

15809 1994 JS

Almost indestructibly strong; a highly resolute compelling energy; unwavering; original or unpredictable; a cunning sleeper cell strategist who unleashes all inhibitions and strikes like a meteor at the right moment.

1994 JS is a 3:5 Neptune Resonant, discovered on May 11, 1994 by David C. Jewitt and Jane X. Luu, and measures 121 km in diameter. At the time of discovery, 1994 JS was located at the 27th degree of Scorpio, conjunct Pluto/Ganesa; sextile Uranus in Capricorn; square 2000 OM67/Taurinensis/Hermes/Opportunity in Aquarius. The North Nodes are conjunct Varda and discovery Sun is conjunct Chaos/2001 YJ140/Cerberus at the 21st degree of Taurus.

This is a very special energy because 1994 JS combines a Herculean leverage force with an extraordinary intelligent and utterly unpredictable talent for strategy, along with an underlying urge to make a major impact. 1994 JS is like a dormant cell that can brood on something for decades, mobilizing all its own talents and resources at a certain moment to appear out of nowhere with a huge impact and do what it always knew it had to do. The drive behind it is based half on an intuitively mystical knowledge, and half on not allowing the other side to continue making its point.

The orbital period is 274 years and 69 days.

20161 1996 TR66

Limitation, being or becoming limited; a heavy or high societal position as suffocation; issues with groups and heartfelt connection; isolation.

1:2 Neptune-Resonant 1996 TR66 was discovered by David C. Jewitt, Chadwick A. Trujillo, Jane X. Luu, and Jun Chen on October 8, 1996. The object was located in the third degree of Aries, conjunct the star Deneb Kaitos (Difda); conjunct Saturn/2002 TX300; trine Pluto/Quaoar; sextile Uranus/Damocles; opposite Haumea. This Twotino measures 139 km in diameter.

The interpretation points in the direction of a high social position in which the role in which one finds oneself remains a hard shell between oneself and contact with people.

Characteristics: the cold mountain top; achieving something at the cost of so much that the victory becomes a loss; isolation; affective limitations; deficiency in all areas, also physical, psychological, or mental; what is missing for real group contact or sharing of idealism, often rooted in misplaced pride or a condemning, overly critical attitude; forced changes; working against oneself by being tough; invalidity; creativity that is great but smothered in the bud. Overall, 1996 TR66 is a heavy, concentric, isolating energy that hinders contact with the group feeling as much as it does with the own heart. The challenge lies in cooperation and investing energy in partnerships, mildness in judgment, and destroying one's own oppressive mindsets or social position.

Forensically, 1996 TR66 indicates the sidelined politician or CEO, the VIP who is out of favor with the public; unusual causes of death. If 1996 TR66 is dominantly aspected or very prominently present via a transit or progression during someone's death, always look at the role of drugs or medications and unusual substances in the blood.

The orbital period is 328 years and 230 days.

26308 1998 SM165

Stringency; stringent completion; not announcing or presenting something until it is fully ready; crystallization; over-optimism; metaphysics.

1998 SM165 is a Twotino, meaning a 1:2 Neptune-Resonant, and was discovered on September 16, 1998 by Nichole M. Danzl. 1998 SM165 has a diameter of 287 km and has a moon, S/2001 (26308), that is 96 km in size.

Characteristics: stringency; strict completion; crystallization; perfect finishing; the maturation/completion period; not announcing or presenting anything before it is completely ready; paying attention to every detail; the coupling of stringency with feeling emotionally and personally secure. In negative terms, it could mean depriving oneself of opportunities due to a not-good-enough complex, or announcing things too optimistically and disappointing others when it does not happen. The sword cuts both ways: either it is perfect and ready for presentation, or it is not even close, and the mind confuses the idea with the completed thing.
In a neutral sense, 1998 SM165 suggests an inclination to translate complex metaphysical questions or situations into more understandable terms for a broader audience. The overall tone of 1998 SM165 is about making things

crystallize clearly (North Nodes in Virgo). Transneptunian.astrology.blogspot links 1998 SM165 to that which needs to remain hidden until it is ready. The area where the energy of this Twotino can be most manifest is that of the 3rd house-9th house axis, so the information, knowledge and communication axis, and the area of spending, publishing, dreaming, transportation, export, travel, brothers, sisters, and the immediate neighborhood.

Its orbital period is 326 years and 189 days.

69988 1998 WA31

The conscious awareness and realization of one's subjective reality in contrast to an imposed and controlling default consensus; resisting being controlled or owned by the state or a system; confronting deep-seated fears; self-sublimation, self-elevation.

1998 WA31 is a 2:5 Neptune resonance object, discovered on November 18, 1998 by Marc William Buie. The object has a diameter of 147 km.

Characteristics: becoming aware and realizing one's own subjective reality in relation to an imposed and controlling default consensus; resisting being heavily controlled or owned by the state or a system; anti-Big Brother; confronting one's deepest subconscious fears; initiating a process of self-sublimation, improvement, or self-realization with a David versus Goliath feeling as a starting point; self-affirmation and formation into a status of autonomous authority achieved in a certain field.

Forensic: whales that strand and die on the beach or are killed for "scientific research"; big lies used to achieve a goal or gain freedom; fraud in the aviation or aerospace industry, university or church sphere, which is caught after causing a big mess; gas explosions triggered by an electrical spark, such as pressing a switch; victims of extreme cruel oppression; Guantanamo Bay situations.

The orbital period is 407 years and 325 days.

78799 2002 XW93

A dynamic and progressive doer; willful and determined; successful political campaigning; optimism; a creative mind.

2002 XW93 is a 5:7 Neptune-resonant object that was discovered on December 10, 2002 by the Palomar Observatory. This candidate dwarf planet measures between 565 and 584 km in diameter.

Characteristics: highly dynamic progressive and will-directed energy; optimism; self-confidence; successful political campaigning; creative mind; warns against getting involved with parasites posing as free spirits; affinity for group sex; interest in parapsychology; aims to align inherent great willpower and talent for planning and goal-setting with easy communication; can get carried away in taking personal liberties that go beyond the norm – usually not from selfishness or lack of empathy, but from enthusiasm.

2002 XW93 has a fiery positive energy in which enthusiasm, purposefulness, and willpower fuse with a never-give-up mentality. However, there is an aspect of having to overcome crises regularly. Mark Andrew Holmes has linked this object, which is strongly in contrast with the fiery dynamics, to humiliation, being despised, being unhappy, being depressed, or being obstructed.

During the discovery, 2002 XW93 was in the 15th degree of Gemini, conjunct the star Cursa (Yuh Tsing) in Gemini (the Central; the Golden Spring), conjunct Dimitrov *(coming out of a crisis)* and 2001 YJ140 *(cut the crap!)*. The Sun is in the discovery horoscope conjunct Pluto/Rhiphonos/Flammario in Sagittarius; trine Jupiter in Leo; trine Eris in Aries. Venus and Mars are conjunct Juno in Scorpio; trine Manwë-Thorodor and square 2002 PN34.

Forensically: very fast-rising companies/successful entrepreneurs; athletes; adventurers; survivors; pilots, astronauts.

Bear Grylls, the popular survivalist and adventurer from Discovery Channel who constantly exposes himself to the most perilous situations, has 2002 XW93 conjunct Venus/Typhon; square Hidalgo/Black Moon/Mors-Somnus; opposition Ixion/Taurinensis; sextile Mercury.

The orbital period is 228 years and 131 days.

84522 2002 TC302

Obsession with politics, stressful situations; finding a new consciousness mode that is nourishing for one's own individuation process; learning processes that develop through metacognition.

2002 TC302 is a large red object measuring 543 × 460 km, possibly a dwarf planet, sometimes classified as an SDO, that was discovered on October 9, 2002. 2002 TC302 is a 2:5 Neptune resonance.

Mark Andrew Holmes has linked 2002 TC302 to stress and political context. The discovery chart of 2002 TC302 has a very strongly aspected Pallas, so 2002 TC302 is certainly politically engaged. However, Pallas is not just political, but also altruism, strategy, genius, and humanity. 2002 TC302 strongly positioned definitely makes it politically involved and political issues are often the source of stress. It is not until one has discovered what is nourishing to their own life, something that they ignore until the situation of structurally neglected self-integrity becomes untenable. Interest in politics then turns into an apolitical attitude and aversion to politics. The social involvement remains strong, but one now seeks a different way of exerting influence. Because Orcus aspects the ascendant and cusp 7 in the discovery chart, this shift, based on the demands of one's individual needs against the obsession with political realities and what irritates in the outside world, is inevitable. 2002 TC302, therefore, revolves around restoring the balance of a disrupted 10th house-4th house axis.

2002 TC302 exhibits an aversion to the negative qualities and expressions of the sign Aries and in some horoscopes, a dominant 2002 TC302 leads to investigative journalism or high-level cultural philosophical reports. Once freed from political stalemate and bickering, the holistic contemplative and understanding of time and group consciousness of 2002 TC302 comes to the surface. 2002 TC302 is particularly strong in making clear why attempts to build bridges between different parties, cultures, groups, and generations fail and how it could be different. A certain form of background stress always remains present with a strong 2002 TC302 in the natal chart. Transits of 2002 TC302 in mundane astrology indicate, by sign and aspect, which areas and facets of society are under political pressure for an extended period. On the website transneptunian-astrology.blogspot.nl, 2002 TC302 is linked to the concept of self-regulated learning. In general, this concept refers to learning that is guided by metacognition (thinking about thinking), strategic action (planning, monitoring, and evaluation of personal progress against a standard), and motivation to learn [definition taken from wikipedia].

The orbital period of 2002 TC302 is 410 years and 314 days.

95625 2002 GX32

Greediness; urge to express oneself; overconfidence; Plutonian energy that needs to be refined and only bears fruit late; subjectivity relativization.

2002 GXZ32 is a 3:7 Neptune resonance object with a diameter of approximately 153 km, discovered by Marc William Buie, Amy B. Jordan, and James L. Elliot on April 8, 2002. This object is sometimes classified as an SDO or Centaur.

There is still some uncertainty about this at the time of writing. 2002 GX32 has a fiery, Pluto/Mars-like energy. There is a lot of power, drive, a need for self-expression and passion. Thinking is goal-oriented, persistent and combative, but this energy is so intense that in most cases it can only bear fruit later in life – through its position in the natal chart and aspects – including a great breakthrough or innovative force. Prior to that, it tends to be prone to overconfident undertakings, half-finished work, forcefully established affairs that later crumble due to faulty assumptions or following or even fetishizing a flawed advice from a guru, icon or strong personality. The latter is actually an initial clumsy attempt to break through the confinement in one's own subjectivity, which starts to feel as a growing insecurity and thus irritate. Communication skills and the construction of sufficient mental baggage, expertise and craftsmanship must first be cultivated to leave behind failures resulting from the tendency to act first and think later.

2002 GX32 was discovered in exact minute conjunction with the massive black hole and super galactic center M87, which Philip Sedgwick previously associated with insatiable hunger and needs, while other astrologers relate M87 to future visions or future forecasts. Language is the best form of expression for the mature 2002 GX32.

One of the more challenging aspects to overcome with a dominant 2002 GX32 concerns a high degree of subjectivity. In order to release the enormous power of 2002 GX32 and be able to act purposefully, one must first be very aware of where one holds the own subjective for objective. Confusing oneself with the work done operates otherwise as a paralysis on one's own development. Conversely, one can gain a lot of advantage and produce very authentic work as a fiction author or idiosyncratic writer from this typical tendency of 2002 GX32 – provided one has learned to relativize one's own subjectivity. All of this always depends on the aspecting.

The orbital period is 389 years and 259 days.

137295 1999 RB216

Insight that nihilism leads to a life without motivation and that meaning is just as important as oxygen; human being versus mechanization/technocratization; overcognition versus faith issues and spiritual doubt; forced or failing nihilism; the comprehensive understanding of making something coherent with the details.

1999 RB216 is a 1:2 Neptune-Resonant, discovered on September 8, 1999 by Chad Trujillo, David C. Jewitt, and Jane X. Luu. This Twotino measures 153 km in diameter.

Characteristics: legitimizing "God" in the human situation and reason; nature versus mechanization/technocratization; over-cognition versus issues of faith and spiritual doubt; prophetic insight into the dichotomy between technological progress and substantive human progress; seeing and understanding the socio-metaphysical implications of the rise of the technical, artificial in life; dogmatic, materialistic humanism or derailing pragmatism; karmic insight into processes and personalities; forced or failing nihilism; understanding that nihilism leads to a motivationless life and that meaning is just as important as oxygen; Luciferian consciousness, fallen angel syndrome; freedom or being trapped in correlation to food and reserves; making something comprehensive by getting the details right; wanting to reconcile spiritual holism with practical, concrete life and the concepts underlying everyday events; the approach that "God" is a verb; ultra-Cartesianism or anti-Cartesianism; "God" is dead versus "God" is complex; doubt about the existence of "God" as an identity conflict that must be purged until a new spiritual grounding is achieved to (re)connect with the exploitation of one's core capacity and belief in oneself. Negative: conforming the soul to a kind of fear contraction in accordance with over-analysis, technology, or their deformed manifestations.

Forensic: engineers dealing with technology and ethics.

The orbital period is 325 years and 270 days.

118378 1999 HT11

Experiencing the immanent divine, immanent spirituality; wiccans.

1999 HT11 was discovered on April 17, 1999 by the Kitt Peak National Observatory (KPNO). It is a 4:7 Neptune Resonant with a diameter of 134 to 146 km.

1999 HT11 appears to be associated with an immanent experience of spirituality, i.e., spirituality that is felt and lived in the here and now, as opposed to the conventional approach of the spiritual as something transcendent.

Forensically: the Shechinah; Wiccans; apostates from state religious systems that mix the spiritual with matters that have nothing to do with it, and therefore no longer provide satisfaction in this area.

Its orbital period is 328 years and 120 days.

119979 2002 WC19

Replacing dualism with complementarity; transcending black-and-white judgments.

2002 WC19 was discovered on November 16, 2002, by the Palomar Observatory. 2002 WC19 is a 1:2 Neptune Resonant object (Twotino) and it is possibly a dwarf planet. The estimated diameter is 338 km to 440 km.

Characteristics: a tendency towards paralyzing or depressing black-and-white thinking and transcending it by thinking not in duality but in complementarity and synergy; racism, discrimination; political grandstanding that perishes due to pride and radicalism; great creative power released when polarizing judgments are set aside.

Its orbital period is 332 years and 244 days.

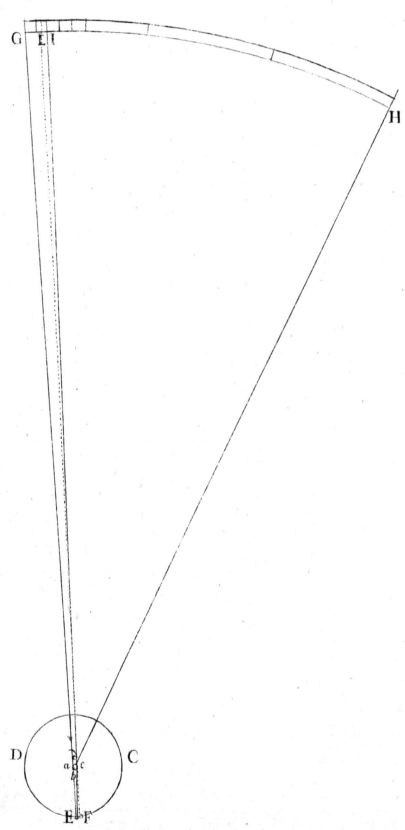

APPENDIX

GLOSSARY OF TERMS

USED IN ASTEROID ASTROLOGY

AE or AU

The astronomical unit (AE or AU) is a unit of distance that is almost equal to the average distance between the Earth and the Sun, approximately 149.6 million kilometers. Since September 2012, the astronomical unit has been defined as exactly 149,597,870,700 meters. This unit is used in astronomy to indicate distances in space, allowing them to be compared with the "radius" of the Earth's orbit around the Sun.

Albedo

Albedo is a measure of how reflective a celestial body, such as a planet or a Moon, is. It is the ratio of the amount of light that an object reflects compared to the amount of light that hits it. A high albedo means that the object reflects a lot of light, while a low albedo means that it absorbs more light. The albedo of an object can vary depending on its surface properties, such as its color, texture, and composition af an asteroid, Moon or planet.

Aphelion & Perihelion

The *aphelion* is the point in the orbit of a planet or other object that revolves around the Sun in an elliptical orbit and is farthest from the Sun. Some objects, especially comets, follow parabolic or even hyperbolic orbits and do not have an aphelion. The counterpart to the aphelion is the perihelion, where the orbit comes closest to the Sun.

The *perihelion* is the point in the orbit of a planet or other object that revolves around the Sun, which is closest to the Sun. Objects with an elliptical orbit also have an aphelion, where the orbit reaches the greatest distance from the Sun.

Asteroid

In previous centuries, it was not known what these celestial bodies were. They were therefore called asteroids (little stars) because they appeared to be like little stars in the sky. The term asteroid is still in use in most languages as a result. In the Dutch language area, the term *planetoïd* (little planet), which is technically more correct, is now preferred in the academic world – not among astrologers.

Asteroids are pieces of matter that, like planets and dwarf-planets, move in an orbit around the Sun. There are now more than 300,000 known asteroids. By far the majority have orbits between the planets Mars and Jupiter. The largest are almost 1000 km in size, but the vast majority are very small. The material is sometimes icy and sometimes rocky, iron or nickel-containing. Asteroids are classified into different classes such as Apollo asteroids, Amor asteroids, asteroid belt or main belt asteroids, Aten asteroids, Mars Trojans, Mars Crossers, Jupiter Trojans, Neptune Trojans, Kuiper belt asteroids and Oort cloud objects.

Amor Asteroids

The Amor asteroids are a group of asteroids that come close to Earth. They are named after the first discovered Amor asteroid, Amor. The Amor asteroids approach the Earth's orbit from the outside but do not cross it. Most Amor asteroids cross Mars' orbit. The two moons of Mars, Deimos and Phobos, are possibly Amor asteroids that have been captured by the Red Planet. The most well-known Amor asteroid is Eros. An Amor asteroid must meet three criteria:

1. An Amor asteroid comes within 0.30 AU of the Earth's orbit.
2. The asteroid's orbit must be outside the Earth's orbit.
3. The asteroid's orbit cannot cross the Earth's orbit. This takes into account the fact that the Earth's orbit varies between 0.983 and 1.016 AE from the Sun.

Apollo asteroids

The Apollo asteroids are a group of asteroids named after the first discovered Apollo asteroid, (1862) Apollo. The orbits of Apollo asteroids cross that of the Earth, with an elliptical orbit whose semi-major axis is greater than that of Earth. Some can come very close to Earth, posing a potential danger to the planet (see Earth-crosser). The closer the value of the semi-major axis of the asteroid is to that of Earth, the smaller the eccentricity of the orbit must be to intersect. Probably an asteroid of 17 meters from the Apollo group fell on the Russian city of Chelyabinsk on February 15, 2013. The largest known Apollo asteroid is (1866) Sisyphus, with a diameter of about 8.5 kilometers.
More than 1400 Apollo asteroids are known, and an updated list can be found at http://www.minorplanetcenter.org/iau/lists/Apollos.html.

Aten asteroids

This group, like the Apollo and Amor asteroids, is a subclass of Earth-crossing asteroids. Aten asteroids are a group of asteroids that come close to the Earth, named after the first discovered Aten asteroid, Aten (January 7, 1976). Their orbit around the Sun has a semi-major axis of less than one astronomical unit (AU). Almost all Aten asteroids have an aphelion greater than one AU. Aten asteroids whose aphelion is entirely within the orbit of Earth are called Apohele asteroids.

Binary Centaur

This group (Binary Centaurs) includes Ceto and Typhon. Typhon and Ceto were given this centaur extension as objects that move in an unstable, non-resonant orbit within which the perihelion is just within the orbit of Neptune. Sometimes these bodies are called SDO-centaurs.

Centaurs

The Minor Planet Center (MPC) defines Centaurs as bodies with a perihelion beyond the orbit of Jupiter and a semi-major axis smaller than that of Neptune. Centaurs have an unstable non-resonant orbit and are mostly composed of ice. In behavior, they seem to be somewhere between a comet and an asteroid. Our solar system is estimated to have about 44,000 Centaurs with a diameter larger than 1 km. Binary Centaurs and Damocloids are separate classes. Astrology has been working with Chiron for some time. However, the largest Centaur is Chariklo. Astrologically, Centaurs are often associated with disruptive effects, wounds (psychological or physical), deformities, sudden positive or negative changes, deep reflection, blind spots, healing abilities, marginal phenomena, or creative border areas. A Centaur disrupts homeostasis and keeps the world in motion with chaotic energy. Like Saturn, Chariklo has rings, and there is strong evidence that Chiron also has rings. Chiron and Echeclus are half-comets. Echeclus has a thin tail (coma). The name Centaur was chosen for this group because they are neither asteroids nor comets, but have characteristics of both, like the mythical centaur, half human and half horse.

Comet

The word comet comes from the Greek word for "long-haired." Comets are relatively small celestial bodies that revolve in often highly elliptical orbits around a star and consist of ice, gas, and dust. When a comet comes close enough to a star and becomes warmer, part of the matter it is made of sublimates to form a so-called coma (gas cloud) and/or a comet tail. Often comets have two tails: a plasma tail and a dust tail, both facing away from the star or Sun. The solid part of the comet is the comet nucleus and can have a diameter of 1 to 50 kilometers. The length of the coma around it can vary greatly: from 100,000 to 1,000,000 kilometers long (up to more than 150 million kilometers long). The orbital period around the star can range from a few years (e.g. comet Encke) to many thousands of years.

Cubewano

The Cubewanos form a group of asteroids in the Kuiper Belt beyond the orbit of Pluto. Their distance from the Sun is between 41 and 48 AU, and their orbital period around the Sun is 260 to 330 years. Their orbits are relatively circular (with a small orbital eccentricity). To be classified as a Cubewano, the asteroid must be quite large (at least about 100 km in diameter). See introduction in this book for more.

Cybele asteroids

Cybele asteroids are likely all formed from the same celestial body that broke apart in the past. The group is named after the asteroid Cybele. Sylvia, which also belongs to the group, and Cybele are the eighth and ninth largest asteroids in the Main Belt, with diameters of 286 and 273 km, respectively. They are located in the outer region of the Main Belt and the axis between their perihelion and aphelion ranges from 3.24 to 3.7 AE. Most of them belong to the C-type of the Tholen classification and are made of dark, carbonaceous material.

Damocloids, ex-comets, and retrograde asteroids

The best-known Damocloids are Damocles, (127546) 2002 XU93, and the retrograde-Centaur Dioretsa. Hidalgo appears astrologically to be a small Damocloid and is likely also a Damocloid. Damocloids are characterized by a very eccentric orbit, a reddish color, and behaving like comets without a tail (coma). The average diameter is 8 km, and there are about a hundred bodies that are candidates for this class. (65407) 2002 RP120 is a Damocloid, a retrograde asteroid, and an SDO.

In addition to the above and (20461) Dioretsa, more than 60 retrograde asteroids have been discovered. Some of them have ephemeris numbers:
(342842) 2008 YB3
(65407)   2002 RP120
(336756) 2010 NV1
(343158) 2009 HC82 (NEO)
(330759) 2008 SO218

There are different types of ex-comets:
4015   Wilson-Harrington (Apollo asteroid)
2060   Chiron (Centaur)
60558   Echeclus (Centaur)
Pizarro   (7968 Elst-Pizarro) First classified as a comet and now a Main Belt
          asteroid.

118401   LINEAR (Main Belt asteroid and comet with occasional coma)
3552   Don Quixote (Amor asteroid, Mars and Jupiter crosser; exhibits
          weak coma)

Astrologically, there is a strong suspicion that these outlier groups can cause significant changes, disturbances, and fluctuations. Given the fact that Damocles was conjunct with the USSR's Radix-Sun in the year it completely fell apart and became various independent states, a precise study of these objects is very interesting. The year 2015 was dominated by Damocles and Hidalgo in the annual horoscope. In this year, faith in the established order and the stability of the established order simultaneously reached a low point. This was true both in terms of citizens versus the system (the whole bank discussion) and, for example, at the EU level, where Greece began to isolate itself from the iron rule dictatorship.

Detached Objects

Detached Objects are SDOs whose perihelion is outside the gravitational pull of Neptune and the other planets. This means that they are detached from the solar system while also being part of it. If the perihelion is further than 50 AU (75 AU according to another definition) from the Sun, we speak of *Sednoids*, named after (90377) Sedna. There are nine Detached Objects discovered, including Sedna, (120132) 2003 FY128, (148209) 2000 CR105, (48639) 1995 TL8, (145480) 2005 TB190, 2000 CR105, and (Buffy) 2004 XR190. (15874) 1996 TL66 with an orbital period of more than 769 years still undergoes an influence from Neptune and falls just outside this category as a kind of boundary guard. (225088) Snow White / 2007 OR10 has a 3:10 resonance with Neptune but is currently moving further from the Sun than Sedna and Eris. *See also under Sednoids.*

Earth-crosser or Near Earth Object (NEA)

An Earth-crosser is an asteroid with an orbit around the Sun that crosses or comes very close to crossing the orbit of Earth. In general, asteroids have orbits outside that of Mars, so Earth-crossers are exceptions. In English, they are referred to as NEOs (Near Earth Orbit/Objects) or NEAs (Near Earth Asteroids), with a definition that requires less strict criteria for actually intersecting with the Earth's orbit. Earth-crossers represent a potential disaster, as such a body can potentially collide with the Earth. This is a daily occurrence for meteoroids, which either burn up in the Earth's atmosphere as shooting stars or cause a meteorite impact. The chance of a sufficiently large asteroid causing a disaster within the next hundred years is present, but very small.

There are likely around a thousand Earth-crossers with a diameter greater than 1 km. Earth-crossers can be found in the classes of Aten, Apollo, and Amor asteroids.

Haumea Family

The Haumea Family, named after Haumea, consists of a unique group of TNO objects consisting mainly of ice that are thought to have originated from a collision between two bodies. Haumea, a rugby ball shaped dwarf planet, is a large object measuring $2100 \times 1680 \times 1074$ km.

Hilda asteroids

A large group of asteroids in a 2/3 resonance with Jupiter between the orbit of Jupiter and the Trojans and the Main Asteroid Belt at a distance between 3.5 and 4.2 AU from the Sun. The asteroid (153) Hilda, after which the group is named, was discovered on November 2, 1875, by Johann Palisa. It is a large, dark asteroid made mostly of carbon with a diameter of 170 km and an orbital period of 7.9 years.

Jupiter Trojans

The Jupiter Trojans consist of two giant clouds of asteroids in Jupiter's orbit, located approximately 60 degrees away from the planet. They are divided into Trojans or the Trojan camp, and Greeks or the Greek camp, named after the Trojan War from Homer's Iliad. Various Jupiter Trojans are currently being studied from an astrological perspective. Hector, Achilles, Nestor, and Agamemnon, for example, are asteroids from the Greek camp. Patrocles, Laocoon, Paris, and Priamus are some of the asteroids from the Trojan camp. There are an estimated 160,000 to 240,000 Jupiter Trojans with diameters larger than 2 km and about 600,000 with diameters larger than 1 km. The Jupiter Trojans border the Hilda asteroids, which move in resonance with Jupiter between the Main Asteroid Belt and Jupiter's orbit. The average orbital period of Jupiter Trojans is just under 12 years. The largest Trojan asteroids are: 624 Hektor (225 km), 911 Agamemnon (167 km), 1437 Diomedes (164 km), 1172 Aeneas (143 km), 617 Patroclus (141 km), 588 Achilles (135 km), 1173 Anchises (126 km), and 1143 Odysseus (126 km).

Kuiper belt

The Kuiper belt, or Kuiper belt, is a belt of billions of comet-like objects made of rock and ice called trans-Neptunian objects, located beyond the orbit of Neptune. The belt is located 30 AU to 50 AU away from the Sun.

Kuiper belt object
See TNO (Trans-Neptunian object).

Neptune Resonant
In the realm of the Kuiper Belt, many objects are categorized and studied based on their resonance with the planet Neptune. Resonance refers to a specific orbital relationship between an object and Neptune, where the gravitational interactions between the two bodies create a stable pattern over long periods of time. One example of such a resonance is the 2:3 resonance, also known as the "Plutino" population. Objects in this resonance complete two orbits around the Sun for every three orbits Neptune completes. The most famous member of this group is dwarf-planet Pluto-Charon, which led to the discovery and subsequent classification of other Plutinos such as Orcus and Ixion. Another resonance is the 1:2 resonance, known as the "Twotino" population. Objects in this resonance complete one orbit for every two orbits Neptune completes. Eris, the dwarf planet that triggered the reclassification of Pluto, is a prominent member of the Twotino group.

There are several larger Neptune-resonant groups of object. The kind of resonance has of course a relation with the average orbital time (data status of 2020):

1:1	resonance	(*Neptune Trojans*, period ~164.8 years)
4:5	resonance	(period~205 years)
3:4	resonance	(period~220 years)
2:3	resonance	(*Plutinos*, period ~247.94 years)
3:5	resonance	(period ~275 years)
4:7	resonance	(period ~290 years)
1:2	resonance	(*Twotinos*, period ~330 years)
3:7	resonance	(period ~385 years)
2:5	resonance	(period ~410 years)
1:3	resonance	(period ~500 years)
2:7	resonance	(*Dziewanna*, period~580 years)
3:10	resonance	(Gonggong, period ~549 years)

Other discovered Neptune resonances with less than 10 objects are:

5:8	resonance	(period ~264 years)
7:12	resonance	(period ~283 years)
5:9	resonance	(period ~295 years)
6:11	resonance	(period ~303 years)
5:11	resonance	(period ~363 years)

4:9	resonance	(period ~370 years)
5:12	resonance	(period ~395 years)
3:8	resonance	(period ~440 years)
4:11	resonance	(period ~453 years)
4:13	resonance	(period ~537 years)
3:10	resonance	(period ~549 years)
2:7	resonance	(period ~580 years)
3:11	resonance	(period ~606 years)
1:4	resonance	(period ~660 years)
5:21	resonance	(period ~706 years)
2:9	resonance	(period ~730 years)
1:5	resonance	(period ~825 years)
2:11	resonance	(period ~909 years)
1:6	resonance	(period ~1000 years)
1:9	resonance	(period ~1500 years)

The *Cubewanos*, also known as Classical Kuiper Belt Objects (KBOs), do not possess a specific resonance with Neptune. They are characterized by their relatively stable and non-resonant orbits that are not strongly influenced by Neptune's gravitational interactions.

The *Hildas* (part of the *Main-belt Asteroids*) are specifically in a 3:2 resonance with Jupiter, meaning they complete three orbits around the Sun for every two orbits that Jupiter completes. The *Jupiter Trojans* are in 1:1 resonance with Jupiter.

Oort cloud
The Oort cloud is a zone around our solar system at a distance between 2000 and 5000 AU, although some astronomers estimate the outer boundary at 100,000 to 200,000 AU. Sedna is one of the few newcomers whose habitat is primarily the Oort cloud.

Orb
In astrology, an "orb" refers to the allowable range of degrees within which a planetary aspect or alignment is considered significant. It represents the margin of error or tolerance for the precision of the aspect. The orb determines how close the planets or points need to be in terms of their degree positions to form a valid aspect in an astrological chart. In asteroid astrology, specific rules regarding orbs are observed. Based on years of observation, I have concluded that when interpreting birth charts, it is advisable to use an orb width of no

more than 1 degree. There is a slight exception for Plutinos and Eris, where a maximum of 2 degrees may be considered (reduced to 1 degree for transits). For transiting asteroids in general, the influence typically begins half a degree before the exact aspect and extends half a degree after. This results in a total observation span of one degree. Adhering to these rules is crucial for obtaining accurate results in asteroid astrology, as it helps minimize the interference of other influences. Among the aspects, the conjunction, square, trine, and opposition hold the greatest significance and should be given priority in analysis.

Orbital period

The orbital period, also known as the revolution period, represents the duration it takes for a celestial object to complete one full orbit around another object. This concept is commonly applied in astronomy to describe the orbital motion of various celestial bodies such as planets, asteroids, moons, exoplanets, or binary star systems. It can also refer to the time required for a satellite to complete one orbit around a planet or moon. In general, the orbital period is determined by a complete 360° revolution of one celestial body around its primary object. For instance, in the case of Earth, it refers to the time it takes for our planet to complete one orbit around the Sun. In astronomy, the orbital periods are typically expressed in units of time, such as hours, days, or years, depending on the specific context and the scale of the orbiting objects.

Planet

A planet in our solar system is a celestial body that:
1. is in orbit around the Sun
2. has enough mass to overcome the internal forces of its own body with its own gravity, thus achieving hydrostatic equilibrium (in other words, it behaves like a fluid and is therefore almost round)
3. has cleared the area around its orbit of other objects.

The above definition was adopted at the IAU conference in August 2006 to classify celestial bodies within our solar system. This is why Pluto lost its status as a planet. If conditions 1 and 2 are met but not condition 3, the celestial body in question is called a dwarf planet. Pluto, Ceres, and Eris are examples of this.

Dwarf planet

A dwarf planet is a category of planet-like celestial bodies. It is related to the definition of a planet adopted by the International Astronomical Union (IAU) since August 24, 2006. According to the definition of the IAU Congress, dwarf planets are celestial bodies that:

- orbit the Sun and do not produce energy through nuclear fusion (unlike stars)
- have enough mass to become (almost) spherical through their own gravity and thus are in hydrostatic equilibrium (unlike smaller asteroids)
- have not cleared their orbit of other objects
- are not a satellite.

The third condition distinguishes between our classical planets and dwarf planets. Pluto, Eris, Makemake, Haumea, and Ceres are bodies that fall into this new category. The discussion of being spherical or almost spherical is a difficult one. Vesta, Pallas, and Hygiea are almost round and also meet the other criteria of the IAU. Initially, these three asteroids were considered planets from the year of their discovery until 1850.

Plutino

In astronomy, a Plutino is a dwarf planet or asteroid located beyond the orbit of the planet Neptune (a trans-Neptunian object) that has a 2:3 orbital resonance with this planet. The dwarf planet Pluto is the largest known representative of this group. Plutinos are located in the inner part of the Kuiper Belt; their average distance from the Sun is between 39 and 40 AU. The eccentricity of their orbits is quite large (usually between 0.1 and 0.3; Pluto: 0.249), and their orbits are often strongly inclined with respect to the ecliptic (orbital inclinations up to 40°; Pluto: 17°). The minimum size to qualify as a plutino is usually set at a few hundred kilometers in diameter. Known Plutinos include Pluto, Orcus, 2003 AZ84, Ixion, and Huya.

Tholen Classification

The Tholen classification is a classification system for asteroids based on their chemical composition expressed in main classes, subtype groups, and smaller classes. The Tholen classification was established after a broadband spectrum survey, the Eight-Color Asteroid Survey (ECAS), combined with albedo analysis, carried out in the 1980s, in which the light spectra of 978 asteroids were analyzed. The albedo of an object is its reflectivity, defined as the ratio of the amount of incident electromagnetic radiation to the amount of reflected radiation. This ratio depends primarily on the material of the object, but also on the wavelength of the radiation. Visible light is usually assumed without further indication.

The main classes are divided into:

> **C-GROUP** [dark carbon rich objects]
  • **B-Type asteroids** (2 Pallas)
  • **F-Type asteroids** (704 Interamnia)
  • **G-Type asteroids** (1 Ceres)
  • **C-type asteroids** (10 Hygeia)

> **S-type asteroïden** [Silicon-rich, rocky objects] (15 Eunomia, 3 Juno)

> **X-GROUP** [metallic objecs]
  • **M-Type asteroids** (16 Psyche)
  • **E-Type asteroids** (44 Nysa, 55 Pandora) – high albedo
  • **P-Type asteroids** (259 Aletheia, 190 Ismene; CP: 324 Bamberga)
    – low albedo

The smaller classes are:
> **A-type asteroids** (246 Asporina)
> **D-type asteroids** (624 Hektor)
> **T-type asteroids** (96 Aegle)
> **Q-type asteroids** (1862 Apollo)
> **R-type asteroids** (349 Dembowska)
> **V-type asteroids** (4 Vesta)

TNO
Abbreviation for Trans-Neptunian Object. Many newcomers have been
discovered in the Kuiper Belt and fall under the category of TNO. Under the
main category TNO or Kuiper Belt Objects, celestial bodies are located at an
average distance of between 30 and 55 AU from the Sun.
These mainly include:
• Plutinos (average distance from the Sun 39-40 AU),
• Cubewanos (average distance from the Sun 41-48 AU) and
• SDOs (average distance from the Sun 48 AU).

Binary Centaurs such as Ceto and Typhon form a separate class. Sedna is
located very far from the Sun (perihelion 76 AU, aphelion 943 AU, with an
orbital period of approximately 11,500 years). Sedna is also an Oort Cloud
object.

Scattered Disk Objects (SDO)

Scattered Disk Objects (SDOs) are a group of asteroids in the outer regions of the solar system. Their orbit around the Sun is greater than 330 years (two or more times that of the planet Neptune), the average distance to the Sun is 48 AU or more, while the closest distance to the Sun is near the orbit of Neptune, usually somewhere between 28 and 40 AU. The orbits are quite elliptical: the orbital eccentricity is between 0.3 and 0.96 - the wider the orbit, the more elliptical (this is an automatic consequence of the fact that the perihelion must lie near the orbit of Neptune). The orbital plane is often significantly inclined to the ecliptic (inclination up to 44°). About one hundred Scattered Disk Objects have been discovered since 1995, the most famous and largest being Eris (estimated diameter 2400 km).

Sednoids

Currently, only four Sednoids have been identified and named: 90377 Sedna, 2012 VP113, 541132 Leleākūhonua (2015 TG387) and 2021 RR205. However, scientists suspect that many more Sednoids exist, awaiting discovery and further exploration. What distinguishes sednoids is their perihelion distance, which lies well beyond the Kuiper cliff at 47.8 astronomical units (AU). These objects lie outside an apparently nearly empty gap in the Solar System and have no significant interaction with the planets. They are usually grouped with the detached objects, and all known Sednoids have perihelia greater than 55 AU.

Defining Sednoids precisely has been a subject of ongoing discussion among researchers. One proposed definition suggests that any object with a perihelion greater than 50 AU and a semi-major axis greater than 150 AU could be classified as a Sednoid. However, this definition also encompasses objects like 2013 SY99, which, despite meeting the criteria, is not considered a sednoid but rather belongs to the same dynamical class as 474640 Alicanto, 2014 SR349, and 2010 GB174.

One of the intriguing aspects of Sednoids is that their peculiar orbits cannot be readily explained by the gravitational influence of the giant planets or interactions with galactic tides. If these objects formed in their current positions, their original orbits must have been nearly circular. This circularity would have facilitated the accretion process, allowing smaller bodies to come together and form larger ones. However, the presence of their present elliptical orbits suggests alternative explanations. One hypothesis proposes that the orbits and perihelion distances of sednoids were altered by the gravitational influence of a nearby passing star during the time when our Sun was part of a stellar birth cluster. This gravitational encounter could have "lifted" their orbits to their current configurations. Another possibility is the disruptive effect of an undiscovered planet-sized body beyond the Kuiper-belt, often referred to as *Planet Nine* or *Planet X* (not to be confused with Quaoar). This hypothetical planet's gravitational interactions could have perturbed the Sednoids' orbits and led to their present-day eccentricities.

Stationary asteroids

In astrology, the term "stationary" refers to a specific phenomenon observed in the movement of planets. It occurs when a planet appears to temporarily halt its normal motion along the zodiac before changing direction. During this time, the planet's apparent movement from Earth's perspective becomes very slow, almost imperceptible. There are two types of stationary points: "stationary direct" and "stationary retrograde."

Stationary Direct: This occurs when a planet, after a period of retrograde motion, comes to a stop before transitioning to direct motion. From Earth, it appears as if the planet has paused in its retrograde path and is about to move forward again.

Stationary Retrograde: This happens when a planet, after moving in direct motion, slows down and comes to a stop before transitioning to retrograde motion. It appears as if the planet has temporarily halted its forward movement and is about to start moving backward in the zodiac.

Stationary points are considered significant in astrology because they intensify the energy and influence of the planet involved. It is believed that when a planet, dwarf planet or asteroid is stationary, its energies become very concentrated and potent, amplifying its effects on individuals and events.

Stationary asteroids and dwarf planets can – just like planets – indicate important shifts, turning points, or periods of heightened intensity in various areas of life depending on the asteroid or dwarf planet involved! In a birth chart they can be a, usually neglected, but very dominant force.

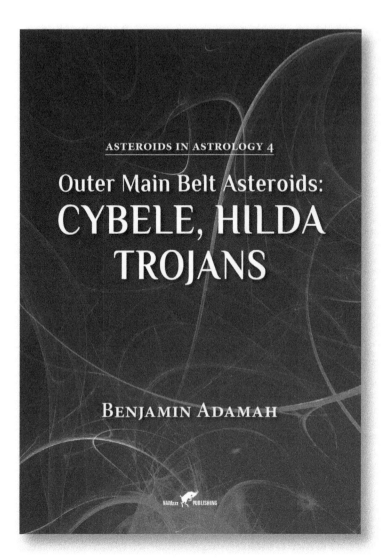

ASTEROIDS IN ASTROLOGY 4

Outer Main Belt Asteroids:
CYBELE, HILDA
TROJANS

BENJAMIN ADAMAH

VAMzzz PUBLISHING

COMING SOON:
Cybele, Hilda & Trojans
Asteroids in Astrology 4

PAPER BOOKS

VAMzzz Publishing is a company that preserves historical occult books and produces new and revised editions in various categories such as Magic & Witchcraft, Secret Rites & Societies, Demonology, Celtic & Mythology, and New Astrology.

Our books are written by highly qualified academic researchers or experts in specific fields of esoteric knowledge, craft, or practice. Many of the revised titles include a Post Scriptum with additional information about the author or subject.

Our reproductions of classic texts differ from others in two important ways. Firstly, we have chosen not to rely on OCR (Optical Character Recognition) technology, as we believe that this often results in poor quality books that are littered with typos and other errors. Secondly, in cases where the original text contains images, such as portraits, maps, or sketches, we have taken great care to preserve the quality of these illustrations, ensuring that they accurately reflect the original artefact. By preserving and sharing these works, we can gain a deeper understanding of our cultural heritage and the rich history of human thought and creativity that has come before us.

In addition to publishing books, VAMzzz Publishing also offers FREE articles on various occult topics, including Afro-American magic, folklore, and New Astrology on our blog. You are welcome to visit vamzzz.com/blog and explore these subjects further.

VAMzzz Publishing
P.O. Box 3340
1001 AC Amsterdam
The Netherlands
vamzzz@protonmail.com
www.vamzzz.com

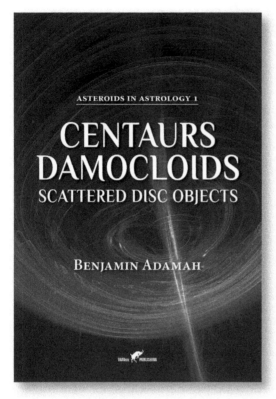

**Centaurs, Damocloids &
Scattered Disc Objects**
Asteroids in Astrology 1
162 pages • Hardcover
ISBN 9789492355409

Challenging the astrological status
quo, this book discusses the fascinating
astrological significance of no less
than 85 Centaurs and Centaur related
asteroids like Scattered Disc Objects
(SDOs) & Detached Objects, Damocloids,
retrograde Asteroids and (ex-) Comets.
Astronomy positions these unstable
objects with their unusual orbits at
the forefront of the evolutionary shifts in our Solar System. Analogue with this astronomical status,
the astrological newcomers described in this book are vital for a true understanding of out-of-
the-box thinking people, as well as complex Zeitgeist-issues and actual mundane phenomena.

Centaurs are of major psychological importance, and as is the case with the first discovered Centaur
Chiron, most of them are about healing and psycho-synthesis. Thus they intrinsically deal with the
converging of opposed, often extreme characteristics into a flow of productive synergy and creative
power. See Nessus, Pylenor, Pholus, Hylonome, Bienor, Crantor, Thereus, Asbolus, to mention but a
few. We have already used the now "standardized" Chiron (218 km in diameter) for years, but why
are many much bigger objects like SDO / dwarf planet Eris (diameter of 2326 km) still ignored?

See Eris' role in great demonstrations and (with Typhon) in major disasters like Fukushima. Can we
truly understand the disintegration of the former USSR while skipping Damocles, the NSA without
2002 RP120, or Edward Snowden without Kondojiro? Not including SDOs like Eris and 1999 TD10 in
(geo)political astrology is an almost provocative way of jumping to false conclusions. 2000 CO104,
2007 TG422 and 2005 PQ21 shed their (taboo breaking) lights on orgasm and sex, while you'll
be amazed at the application of 1998 BU48, 1996 TL66 and 2001 BL41 in financial astrology...

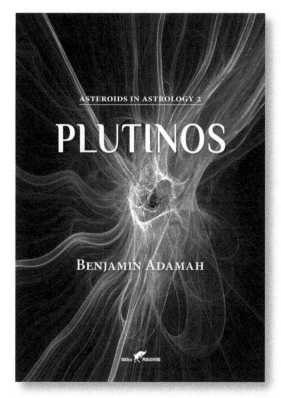

Plutinos
Asteroids in Astrology 2
126 pages • Hardcover
ISBN 9789492355522

Plutinos are asteroids and in some cases dwarf planet candidates, circling around in the inner Kuiper belt, in orbits comparable to the one of Pluto (Pluto-Charon). Astrological research points out that most Plutinos, like their godfather Pluto, exert a compelling force in both personal and mundane horoscopes. They are radical, transforming, confronting, they penetrate the darkness, the blur, or daily life patterns and have a Scorpio-like preference for what you might call soul-mining. They trigger the awareness of slumbering patterns in the depths of our souls and force us to face the truth.

Most Plutinos are "isolating" one or two classic Plutonian keywords, such as: intensifying, dark, transforming, cutting away dead wood, letting go, death, discharging, imploding, violence, criminality, rebellion, dirt, sex, penetration, psychopaths or the occult. Strong transits, to or from these slow moving asteroids, can act as serious turning points in our lives. Negatively, several Plutinos exacerbate those qualities belonging to the darker side of Pluto and its sign Scorpio. All members of this classification fill in many gaps in chart interpretations, adding much to both personal and mundane astrology.

After his 2019 debute on Centaurs, Damocloids and SDO's, Benjamin Adamah now presents the astrological meaning of 44 Plutinos. Apart from Orcus(-Vanth), Ixion, Arawn, Huya, Lempo(-Hiisi), Mors-Somnus and Rhadamantus, 37 other important Plutinos, cataloged by MPC-number, are discussed. This book comes with a special appendix about the chart of the USA and its crucial role within the current world-crisis. This analysis is based on Plutinos and the Black Sun-Diamond axis. A second appendix shows a substantial list of Pluto-Charon aspects with asteroids of several classes which – like the Plutinos – have specific Plutonic features in common with the gatekeeper of our solar system.

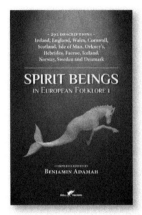

Spirit Beings in European Folklore 1

292 descriptions – Ireland, England, Wales, Cornwall, Scotland, Isle of Man, Orkney's, Hebrides, Faeroe, Iceland, Norway, Sweden and Denmark
250 pages • Paperback • ISBN 9789492355553

Compendium 1 of the Spirit Beings in European Folklore-series covers the northwestern part of the continent where Celtic and Anglo-Saxon cultures meet the Nordic. This book catalogs the mysterious creatures of Ireland, the Isle of Man, England, Wales, Cornwall, Scotland, Hebrides, Orkneys, Faroe Islands, Iceland, Norway, Sweden and Denmark. For centuries, the peoples of these regions have influenced each other in many ways, including their mythologies and folklore. The latter is perhaps most evident in the various species of Brook-horses or Water-horses. These semi-aquatic ghostly creatures come in all kinds of varieties and are typical of the English or Gaelic speaking parts of Europe and Scandinavia. Many other ghostly entities occur only in specific areas or countries. Some even became cultural icons, such as the Irish Leprechaun, the Knockers from Wales, the Scandinavian Trolls and Huldras or the Icelandic Huldufólk. England has its Brownies, several kinds of Fairies and locally famous ghost dogs. Iceland and Scandinavia seem to "specialize" in spirit beings who appear fully materialized, such as the different species of Illveli (Evil Whales) and Draugr, the returning dead.

Spirit Beings in European Folklore 2

228 descriptions – Germany, Austria, Alpine regions, Switzerland, Netherlands, Flanders, Luxembourg, Lithuania, Latvia, Estonia, Finland, Jewish influences
256 pages • Paperback • ISBN 9789492355560

Compendium 2 of the Spirit Beings in European Folklore-series covers the German-speaking parts of Central Europe, the Low Countries, the Baltic region and Finland. Via the Ashkenazi Jews, spirit beings from the Middle East entered Central European culture, which are also included. This originally densely forested part of the continent is particularly rich in nature-spirits and has a wide variety of beings that dwell in forests and mountainous areas (Berggeister) or act as atmospheric forces. Also dominant are the many field-spirits and variations of Alp-like creatures (Mare, Nightmare). There is an overlap with the Nordic and Eastern European Revenant and Vampire-types, and we find several water- and sea-spirits. Among the German-speaking and Baltic peoples, invoking field-spirits was an integrated part of agriculture, with rites continuing into the early 20th century. The Alpine regions have spirits who watch over cattle. In general, forest-spirits are prominent. Germany has its Moosweiblein and Wilder Mann (Woodwose), the Baltic region has its Mātes, and Finland its Metsän Väki. Then there are ghostly animals, and earth- and house-spirits such as the many kinds of Kobolds, the Dutch Kabouter, and the Kaukas of Prussia and Latvia.

Spirit Beings in European Folklore 3

255 descriptions – Russia, Belarus, Ukraine, Poland, Romania, Hungary, Bulgaria, Czechia, Slovenia, Serbia, Croatia, Albania, Georgia, Turkish regions, Roma-culture

246 pages • Paperback • ISBN 9789492355577

Compendium 3 of the Spirit Beings in European Folklore-series offers an overview of the mysterious, sometimes beautiful and often shadowy entities of the Slavic countries, the Balkans, the Carpathians, Albania, Georgia, and the Turkish and Romani peoples. Many types of Vampires and vampiric Revenants are included – in their original state and purged of later applied disinformation. The undead are prominent in the folklore of Eastern Europe and Albania. Also typical are farm- and household-spirits such as the Domovoy, water-spirits and forest demons like the Russian Leshy, the Chuhaister, or the evil Polish Bełt, who like the Ukrainian Blud, leads travelers off their path until they are lost in the deepest part of the forest. Unique is the Russian Bannik or spirit of the bathhouse. Amongst the Slavs, some 'demons', like the Boginka for example, originally belonged to the pre-Christian pantheon. Eastern Europe, in contrast to its returning dead, is rich in seductive female spirits such as the Romanian Iele, the Russian Russalka, the Vila of the Eastern and Southern Slavs and the Bulgarian Samodiva. Via the Balkans, Greek influences entered Slavic culture, while there are also spirits that intersect Germanic and Nordic folklore.

Spirit Beings in European Folklore 4

270 descriptions – France, Brittany, Wallonia, Portugal, Italy, South Tyrol, Malta, Greece, Spain – Basque Country, Asturias, Catalonia, Cantabria, Galicia, Valencia

250 pages • Paperback • ISBN 9789492355584

Compendium 4 of the Spirit Beings in European Folklore-series covers an area that starts with Wallonia and continues via France and the Pyrenees, through the Iberian Peninsula, to Italy and Greece. This results in a very diverse and colourful collection of spirit beings, due to the many included Basque nature-spirits or Ireluak, the Spanish Duendes, the Celtic spirits of Brittany, the prankster Italian Folletti and the creatures from Greece. Some creatures from Breton folklore are particularly gruesome, such as the hollow-eyed Ankou, the Werewolf-like Bugul-nôz, or the ghostly and Will-o'-the-wisp-like Yan-gant-y-tan, who roams the night roads with his five lit candles. Most Italian ghosts are less gloomy, while the Iberian Peninsula is home to everything ranging from the 'Beauty' to the 'Beast'. Compendium 4 contains – amongst other things – many kinds of dwarf-spirits or Goblins (Lutins, Nutons, Folletti, Farfadettes, Korrigans, Minairons) various seductive and feminine spring creatures, Wild Man-varieties (Basajaunak, Jentilak) and an extensive section on the Incubus-Succubus. It is fascinating to discover how many types of European spirit beings (from Kobold to many female spring-spirits), described in the other Compendiums, can be traced back to creatures from Ancient Greece.